# First World War
### and Army of Occupation
# War Diary
### France, Belgium and Germany

30 DIVISION
90 Infantry Brigade
London Regiment
2/15 Battalion (Civil Service Rifles)
1 June 1918 - 19 October 1919

WO95/2340/3

The Naval & Military Press Ltd
www.nmarchive.com
Published in association with The National Archives

Published by

## The Naval & Military Press Ltd

Unit 10 Ridgewood Industrial Park,

Uckfield, East Sussex,

TN22 5QE England

Tel: +44 (0) 1825 749494

www.naval-military-press.com

www.nmarchive.com

*This diary has been reprinted in facsimile from the original. Any imperfections are inevitably reproduced and the quality may fall short of modern type and cartographic standards.*

© **Crown Copyright**
**Images reproduced by permission of The National Archives, London, England, 2015.**

# Contents

| Document type | Place/Title | Date From | Date To |
|---|---|---|---|
| Heading | WO95/2340 2/15 London (Civil Service Rifles) Jun '18-Oct '19 | | |
| Heading | 30th Division 90th Infy Bde 2-15th London Regt. (P.W.O. Civil Service Rifles) Jun 1918-Oct 1919 From Egypt 60 Div 119 Bde | | |
| Heading | 2/15th London Regt. June 1918 | | |
| Heading | War Diary of 2/15th Battalion London Regt. 1st-30th June 1918 Volume IV | | |
| War Diary | Surafend | 01/06/1918 | 02/06/1918 |
| War Diary | Kantara | 03/06/1918 | 15/06/1918 |
| War Diary | Alexandria | 16/06/1918 | 17/06/1918 |
| War Diary | At. Sea | 18/06/1918 | 23/06/1918 |
| War Diary | Cimino Italy | 24/06/1918 | 24/06/1918 |
| War Diary | On Train | 25/06/1918 | 30/06/1918 |
| Miscellaneous | 2/15th Battalion London Regiment. Operation Order LI. Appendix I | 14/06/1918 | 14/06/1918 |
| Miscellaneous | Battn Orders by Major AW Gaze MC Coy app II | 23/06/1918 | 23/06/1918 |
| Heading | War Diary of the 2/15th Bn. London Regt. (P.W.O. Civil Service Rifles) for the month of July 1918 Volume No. IV | | |
| Heading | War Diary of 2/15th Battalion London Regiment (P.W.O.) Civil Service Rifles. 1st-31st July 1918 Volume IV | | |
| Miscellaneous | | | |
| War Diary | Sheet 27 A.S.E 1/20000 Q.17.b.2.9 | 01/07/1918 | 08/07/1918 |
| War Diary | T.11.a.7.8 | 09/07/1918 | 09/07/1918 |
| War Diary | Map Ref Sheet 27. SE 1/20000 Q.19.b.6.1 | 10/07/1918 | 17/07/1918 |
| War Diary | Q.19.b.6.1 | 18/07/1918 | 31/07/1918 |
| Operation(al) Order(s) | 2/15th Battn. London Regiment. Order No. LII. Appendix I | 07/07/1918 | 07/07/1918 |
| Operation(al) Order(s) | Battalion Orders No. 142 By Major A.C.H. Benke, M.C., Commdg. Appendix II | 08/07/1918 | 08/07/1918 |
| Operation(al) Order(s) | 2/15th Battalion London Regiment Operation Order No. LIII. app III | 25/07/1918 | 25/07/1918 |
| Operation(al) Order(s) | 2/15th Battn. London Regiment. Operation Order No. 54. Appendix IV | 26/07/1918 | 26/07/1918 |
| War Diary | 2/15th Battn. London Regiment. Operation Order No. 55. Appendix V | 29/07/1918 | 29/07/1918 |
| Heading | War Diary of the 2/15th Battalion London Regt., (P.W.O.) Civil Service Rifles) for the month of August, 1918. Vol 3 | | |
| War Diary | R.8.C.9.5 | 01/08/1918 | 02/08/1918 |
| War Diary | Q.19.b.7.1 | 03/08/1918 | 08/08/1918 |
| War Diary | R.9.a.4.5 | 09/08/1918 | 09/08/1918 |
| War Diary | M.22.a.5.4 | 10/08/1918 | 16/08/1918 |
| War Diary | M.22.d.0.9 | 17/08/1918 | 18/08/1918 |
| War Diary | M.22.a.5.4 | 19/08/1918 | 19/08/1918 |
| War Diary | R.8.c.2.7 | 20/08/1918 | 22/08/1918 |
| War Diary | M.22.c.9.9 | 23/08/1918 | 26/08/1918 |
| War Diary | M.22.a.5.4 | 27/08/1918 | 28/08/1918 |

| | | | |
|---|---|---|---|
| War Diary | R.8.c.2.7 | 29/08/1918 | 31/08/1918 |
| Operation(al) Order(s) | 2/15th Battalion London Regt. Operation Order No. LVI. Appendix I | 03/08/1918 | 03/08/1918 |
| Operation(al) Order(s) | 2/15th Battalion London Regt. Operation Order No. LVIII. Appendix II | 09/08/1918 | 09/08/1918 |
| Heading | C.O | | |
| Operation(al) Order(s) | 2/15th Bn. London Regiment. Order No. LIX. Appendix III | 15/08/1918 | 15/08/1918 |
| Miscellaneous | Defence Scheme 2/15th London Regiment. | 16/08/1918 | 16/08/1918 |
| Miscellaneous | Report On New Positions In Locrehof Sector. | 25/08/1918 | 25/08/1918 |
| Operation(al) Order(s) | 2/15th London Regt. Order No. LX Appendix IV | 17/08/1918 | 17/08/1918 |
| Operation(al) Order(s) | 2/15th Battalion London Regiment. Order No. LXI. Appendix V | 19/08/1918 | 19/08/1918 |
| Map | Enlargement of M 21 b.d. & 22.a.b.c.d. Ref Map Kemmel 1: 10,000 | | |
| Operation(al) Order(s) | 2/15th Battn. London Regiment. Order No. LXII. Appendix VI | 21/08/1918 | 21/08/1918 |
| Operation(al) Order(s) | 2/15th Battn. London Regiment. Operation Order No. LXIII. Appendix VII | 25/08/1918 | 25/08/1918 |
| Miscellaneous | Battalion Orders By Lt-Col. A.W. Gaze, M.C. Cmmdg. Appendix VIII | 27/08/1918 | 27/08/1918 |
| Heading | 2/15th London Regt. September 1918 | | |
| Heading | War Diary of 2/15th Battn London Regt for September 1918 Vol 4 | | |
| War Diary | Sheet 28. S.W.M. 1/20000 M.16.b.1.9 | 01/09/1918 | 02/09/1918 |
| War Diary | N.31.d | 03/09/1918 | 03/09/1918 |
| War Diary | N.33.a.7.5 | 04/09/1918 | 05/09/1918 |
| War Diary | N.31.D | 06/09/1918 | 09/09/1918 |
| War Diary | M.21.a.5.4 | 10/09/1918 | 19/09/1918 |
| War Diary | T.10.b.6.7 | 20/09/1918 | 26/09/1918 |
| War Diary | T.6.b.7.1 | 27/09/1918 | 27/09/1918 |
| War Diary | T.6.c.7.1 | 28/09/1918 | 29/09/1918 |
| War Diary | O.36.b.3.6 | 30/09/1918 | 30/09/1918 |
| Miscellaneous | To Coy The Battn will relieve Appendix I | 07/09/1918 | 07/09/1918 |
| Miscellaneous | Battn Orders. app II | 08/09/1918 | 08/09/1918 |
| Operation(al) Order(s) | 2/15th Battn. London Regt. Order No. LXIII. App. III | 19/09/1918 | 19/09/1918 |
| Operation(al) Order(s) | Administrative Instructions To Order No. LXIII. | 19/09/1918 | 19/09/1918 |
| Operation(al) Order(s) | Order No. LXIV. app IV | 23/09/1918 | 23/09/1918 |
| Operation(al) Order(s) | Order No. LXV. app V | | |
| Miscellaneous | Amendments to Order No LXV | 26/09/1918 | 26/09/1918 |
| Miscellaneous | Ref F.A 7 | | |
| Miscellaneous | Artillery. Barrage details to Follow | | |
| Miscellaneous | Admin Instrns to Order LXVI | 27/09/1918 | 27/09/1918 |
| Operation(al) Order(s) | Order No LXVI by Major A.C.H Benke M.C. Commdg 2/15 London Rgt app VI | 27/09/1918 | 27/09/1918 |
| Miscellaneous | Amendments to Order No LXVI | | |
| Operation(al) Order(s) | Order No LXVII app VII | | |
| Operation(al) Order(s) | Order No LXVIII app VIII | | |
| Miscellaneous | Battn Orders | 29/09/1918 | 29/09/1918 |
| Heading | War Diary of the 2/15th Battalion London Regiment (P.W.O.) Civil Service Rifles for the month of October, 1918. Volume No. IV Vol 5 | | |
| War Diary | Map Reference Belgium Sheet 28 1/20000 O.36.b.3.7 | 01/10/1918 | 02/10/1918 |
| War Diary | O.27.a | 03/10/1918 | 03/10/1918 |
| War Diary | O.14.d.8.2 | 04/10/1918 | 08/10/1918 |
| War Diary | O.14.b.0.4 | 09/10/1918 | 11/10/1918 |

| | | | |
|---|---|---|---|
| War Diary | Q.13.a.3.7 | 12/10/1918 | 15/10/1918 |
| War Diary | Q.14.b.9.4 | 16/10/1918 | 17/10/1918 |
| War Diary | Q.36.d.5.2 | 18/10/1918 | 18/10/1918 |
| War Diary | M.32.b.6.7 | 19/10/1918 | 19/10/1918 |
| War Diary | S.5.a.3.7 | 20/10/1918 | 20/10/1918 |
| War Diary | T.3.d.1.4 | 21/10/1918 | 31/10/1918 |
| Operation(al) Order(s) | Order No 69. App. I | 01/10/1918 | 01/10/1918 |
| Operation(al) Order(s) | Order No 70 by Lt Col ACH Barks M.C App. II | 12/10/1918 | 12/10/1918 |
| Miscellaneous | Amendments to Order No 70 | 13/10/1918 | 13/10/1918 |
| Diagram etc | Sketch attached to amendment of Operation Order 70 | | |
| Heading | War Diary Of The 2/15th Battalion London Regt (P.W.O., Civil Service Rifles) for the month of November 1918 Volume No. 4 Vol 6 | | |
| War Diary | T.3.d.1.4 | 01/11/1918 | 01/11/1918 |
| War Diary | P.33.b.9.7 | 02/11/1918 | 04/11/1918 |
| War Diary | O.32.c.8.4 | 05/11/1918 | 06/11/1918 |
| War Diary | N.20.d.0.7 | 07/11/1918 | 10/11/1918 |
| War Diary | P.25.c.8.5 | 11/11/1918 | 15/11/1918 |
| War Diary | N.20.c.8.4 | 16/11/1918 | 30/11/1918 |
| Miscellaneous | App I | 10/11/1918 | 10/11/1918 |
| Miscellaneous | App II | 11/11/1918 | 11/11/1918 |
| Heading | H.Q | | |
| Miscellaneous | Battalion Orders By Lieut.-Col. A.C.H. Benke, MC., Cmmdg. app III | 14/11/1918 | 14/11/1918 |
| Operation(al) Order(s) | 2/15th Battn. London Regt. Order No. LXXV. app IV | 29/11/1918 | 29/11/1918 |
| Heading | War Diary of 2/15th Battalion London Regiment (P.W.O.) Civil Service Rifles for December 1918 Vol 7 | | |
| War Diary | Hazebrouck Map Boeseghem | 08/12/1918 | 14/12/1918 |
| War Diary | Sheet 28. W.23.c.1.8 | 01/12/1918 | 01/12/1918 |
| War Diary | Sheet 36a J.3.b.3.8 | 02/12/1918 | 02/12/1918 |
| War Diary | Sheet 36a G.17.b.1.0 | 03/12/1918 | 03/12/1918 |
| War Diary | Hazebrouck Map St Venant | 04/12/1918 | 04/12/1918 |
| War Diary | Boeseghem | 05/12/1918 | 07/12/1918 |
| War Diary | Hazebrouck Map Boeseghem | 15/12/1918 | 25/12/1918 |
| War Diary | Boeseghem | 26/12/1918 | 31/12/1918 |
| Heading | 2/15th Battalion London Regiment. War Diary for the month of January 1919 Vol 8 | | |
| War Diary | Boeseghem | 01/01/1919 | 02/01/1919 |
| War Diary | Coyecque | 03/01/1919 | 03/01/1919 |
| War Diary | Herly-Avesnes | 04/01/1919 | 04/01/1919 |
| War Diary | Estrelles-Estree | 05/01/1919 | 05/01/1919 |
| War Diary | Etaples La Gouffe Camp Letouquet | 06/01/1919 | 11/01/1919 |
| War Diary | Etaples La Gouffe Camp | 12/01/1919 | 14/01/1919 |
| War Diary | Dunkirk | 15/01/1919 | 31/01/1919 |
| Heading | 2/15th Battalion London Regiment War Diary for the month of February Vol 9 | | |
| War Diary | Dunkirk | 01/02/1919 | 28/02/1919 |
| Heading | 2/15 London Regiment. War Diary for March 1919 Vol 10 | | |
| War Diary | Dunkirk | 01/03/1919 | 11/03/1919 |
| War Diary | Dannes | 12/03/1919 | 12/03/1919 |
| War Diary | St Cecile Plage | 13/03/1919 | 31/03/1919 |
| Heading | War Diary 2/15 London Regiment. April 1919. Vol 11 | | |
| War Diary | St Cecile Plage | 01/04/1919 | 30/04/1919 |
| Heading | 2/15 London Regiment. War Diary for May 1919. Vol 12 | | |

| | | | |
|---|---|---|---|
| War Diary | St Cecile Plage | 01/05/1919 | 22/05/1919 |
| War Diary | Abbeville | 23/05/1919 | 23/05/1919 |
| War Diary | St Riquier | 24/05/1919 | 31/05/1919 |
| Heading | 2/15th London Regiment. War Diary for June 1919 Vol 13 | | |
| War Diary | Vauchelles | 01/06/1919 | 30/06/1919 |
| Heading | War Diary for July 1919 2/15th London Regiment. Vol 14 | | |
| War Diary | Vauchelles | 01/07/1919 | 31/07/1919 |
| Heading | War Diary Of The 2/15th. London Regiment (Civil Service Rifles.) For The Month Of August, 1919 (Volume No.) | | |
| War Diary | Vauchelles | 11/08/1919 | 23/08/1919 |
| War Diary | Vauchelles | 01/08/1919 | 31/08/1919 |
| Miscellaneous | To Headquarters Abbeville Sub-Area. | 14/10/1919 | 14/10/1919 |
| Miscellaneous | The Secretary War Office. (SD 2) London. | 18/10/1919 | 18/10/1919 |
| War Diary | Vauchelles | 01/09/1919 | 24/09/1919 |
| War Diary | Abbeville | 25/09/1919 | 29/09/1919 |
| Miscellaneous | Disposal Of Canteen Funds. | 16/09/1919 | 16/09/1919 |
| War Diary | Abbeville | 30/09/1919 | 30/09/1919 |
| Miscellaneous | The Secretary War Office (SD 2) London | 19/10/1919 | 19/10/1919 |
| War Diary | Abbeville | 01/10/1919 | 19/10/1919 |
| Miscellaneous | Headquarters, L. of C. Area. | 07/10/1919 | 07/10/1919 |
| Miscellaneous | O.C. 2/15th London Regt. | 14/10/1919 | 14/10/1919 |

WO 95/2340
2/15 London
(Civil Service Rifles)
Jan '18 - Oct '19

30TH DIVISION
90TH INFY BDE

2-15TH LONDON REGT
(P.W.O. CIVIL SERVICE RIFLES)
JUN 1918 - OCT 1919

FROM EGYPT
60 DIV 179 BDE

Index..........

## SUBJECT.

2/15th London Regt.

| No. | Contents. | Date. |
|---|---|---|
| | June 1918. | |

CONFIDENTIAL

WAR DIARY

of

2/15th Battalion London Regt.

1st - 30th June 1916

Volume IV

Army Form C. 2118.

# WAR DIARY
## or
## INTELLIGENCE SUMMARY.
*(Erase heading not required.)*

Instructions regarding War Diaries and Intelligence Summaries are contained in F. S. Regs., Part II. and the Staff Manual respectively. Title pages will be prepared in manuscript.

| Place | Date | Hour | Summary of Events and Information | Remarks and references to Appendices |
|---|---|---|---|---|
| SURAFEND | 1/6/18 | 0530 | Batt arrival at Surafend | PM |
| " | 2/6/18 | 1500 | Batt less A.T.C. coy's entrained at LUDD for KANTARA. 2100 hrs A.T.C. coy's entrained. | PM |
| KANTARA | 3/6/18 | 0600 | Arrival at KANTARA. | AM |
| " | 4/6/18 | | Physical Training. 2nd Lt S MILLER & 1/c C/S.M. joined for duty. | PM |
| " | 5/6/18 | | " " 2nd Lt W.J. MURRAY rejoined from hospital | PM |
| " | 6/6/18 | | " " | |
| " | 7/6/18 | | | 2nd Lts S L BONNER and V S BURTT joined for duty 7.18.14 |
| " | 8/6/18 | | | 7.19.14 |
| " | 9/6/18 | | Voluntary Church Parade | 7.12.14 |
| " | 10/6/18 | | Gashing & Fitting of Box Respirators | AM |
| " | 11/6/18 | | Nooning | PM |
| " | 12/6/18 | | Lt W.P WEBB joined Advance Party at MARSEILLES | PM |

Army Form C. 2118.

# WAR DIARY
## or
## INTELLIGENCE SUMMARY.
(Erase heading not required.)

Instructions regarding War Diaries and Intelligence Summaries are contained in F. S. Regs., Part II. and the Staff Manual respectively. Title pages will be prepared in manuscript.

| Place | Date | Hour | Summary of Events and Information | Remarks and references to Appendices |
|---|---|---|---|---|
| KANTARA | 17/6/18 | | Training. 222 BORTT posted to B Coy. 2½L WHEELER reported to C Coy. | P.M. |
| " | 18/6/18 | | Gas drill etc. | P.M. |
| " | 19/6/18 | 1800 | Batt entrained for ALEXANDRIA. Strength 30 Officers, 813 Ranks, 11 C.W. CAMPBELL, 2/Lts G.R. HOWARD GRAFTON, H.R.A. CUNNINGHAM, O.S. ALISON, L. BARCLAY, C.H. HODGSON, A.C. McDOWALL & 15 Ranks supplies to accommodation to No 2 I.B. Depot for disposal. | App I P.M. |
| ALEXANDRIA | 20/6/18 | 0445 | Arrived at ALEXANDRIA. Embarked on H.M.T. INDARA at 0700 hrs & moved alongside Quay. | P.M. |
| " | 21/6/18 | | Ships routine. Moved from Quay to Harbour at 10.30 hrs | P.M. |
| AT SEA | 18/6/18 | | Sailed at 13.13 hrs. | P.M. |
| " | 19/6/18 | | " | P.M. |
| " | 20/6/18 | | Usual ship routine. | P.M. |
| " | 21/6/18 | | " | P.M. |
| " | 22/6/18 | | " Submarine first reported chasing at 18.00 hrs | P.M. |
| " | 23/6/18 | | Arrived TARANTO HARBOUR 13.30 hrs. Moved into INNER HARBOUR at 17.00 hrs. Unloading commenced at 21.00 hrs. Capt LEECH & 7 Ranks to hospital. | P.M. |
| " | 23/6/18 | 0130 | Disembarked & proceeded to REST CAMP. CIMINO | P.M. |
| CIMINO ITALY | 24/6/18 | | Entrained for FRANCE at 8.10 from Capt LEECH from hospital. | App II P.M. |
| ON TRAIN | 25/6/18 | | At lunch. Stopped at BARI, then FOGGIA. | P.M. |

Army Form C. 2118.

# WAR DIARY
or
# INTELLIGENCE SUMMARY.

*(Erase heading not required.)*

Instructions regarding War Diaries and Intelligence Summaries are contained in F. S. Regs., Part II. and the Staff Manual respectively. Title pages will be prepared in manuscript.

| Place | Date | Hour | Summary of Events and Information | Remarks and references to Appendices |
|---|---|---|---|---|
| ON TRAIN | 26/9/18 | | Hoffman & CASTELLAMARE & FAENZA | See. |
| " | 27/9/18 | | SAMPIERDARENA & VENTIMIGLIA | " |
| " | 28/9/18 | | MIRAMAS & LG TIEL | " |
| " | 29/9/18 | | PARAY LE MONAL | " |
| " | 30/9/18 | | MALESHERBES & U.S. | " |

A. W. Page. Major
Coy. 2/15th Battalion London Regiment,
(P.W.O.) Civil Service Rifles.

SECRET.

Appendix I

Copy No. 11

## 2/15th Battalion London Regiment.

### OPERATION ORDER LI.

14th June, 1918.

1. The Battalion will entrain at KANTARA to-morrow evening, 15th inst., for ALEXANDRIA, and embark for EUROPE on the 16th inst.

2. The Battalion will form up in Mass on No. 2. Inf. Base Depot parade ground at 16.30 hours. 4 markers per Coy. to report to R.S.M. at 16.10 hrs. at the Orderly Room. All details will parade with their Companies.

3. BAGGAGE.
Blankets, rolled in bundles of 10, and greatcoats in bundles of 6, will be dumped S. of Mess Huts at 06.00 hours, together with Kit Bags.
Officers valises, Orderly Room Boxes, R.A.P. Boxes, Coy. & Cooks Boxes will be dumped at same place at 09.00 hours.
All baggage is to be clearly labelled.
Separate arrangements will be made for the transport of dixies.
Blankets will be re-issued on arrival at ALEXANDRIA.

4. All water bottles will be filled before leaving camp.

5. Rations will be issued on board from and including the dinner meal on day of embarkation.

6. Troops will not detrain on arrival at ALEXANDRIA until ordered to do so.

7. "C" Coy. will provide a loading party of 1 Sgt., 2 Cpls. 25 Ptes., under 2nd Lt. E.N. WHEELER. This party will report to the Q.M. when the Battalion arrives at KANTARA STATION.
"C" Coy. will provide a guard of 1 N.C.O. & 3 men to report to Q.M. at 06.00 hours in full marching order. They will travel with first baggage load and mount guard over baggage on the station.

7(a)

8. O's. C. Coys. will furnish a certificate to the Orderly Room at 16.15 hours that the camp has been left clean and in a sanitary condition.

S. C. HALL,
Capt. & Adjutant.

Issued at 12.00 hours.
Copy No. 1. Major A.C.H. BENKE, M.C.   No. 2. O.C., "A" Coy.
     3. O.C., "B" Coy.                      4. O.C., "C" Coy.
     5. O.C., "D" Coy.                      6. Scout Officer.
     7. Q.M.                                8. M.O.
     9. T.O.                               10. R.S.M.
    11. War Diary.                         12. Retained.
    13. Lt. F.H. DU HEAUME

7(a) ENTRAINING OFFICER. Lieut. F.H. DU HEAUME.
One Officer per Coy. will report to Lieut. F.H. DU HEAUME on arrival at KANTARA STATION.

App II

Batten Orders by                     Sunday
Major AW Gaye MC Cy                  23/6/18.

1. ROUTINE Reveille 0600 Breakfast 0700
             Sick Parade 0830
      Coy on duty  A    next  B
      Officer of the day.  2 Lt B N Wheeler
         next               2 Lt R J Murray

2. WORK Coys will hold rifle inspections.
   The Camp Commandant will inspect
   the Camp at 1100 hrs. Kit will be
   arrayed inside the tent & men will
   fall in outside the tents at 1055 hrs.
   The Officer of the Day will accompany
   the Camp Commandant round the lines.

3. REPOSTING Capt H J G BACK is posted to
   D Coy & will assume command
   23/6/18.
      Lt- 7 W PHELPS is posted to A Coy 15/6/18
      2 Lt A P PITTAM    "    "    A   23/6/18

4. The Batten will entrain tomorrow for
   France. Parade ready to march
   off at 1800 hrs, on ground N of
   Camp. Two markers per Coy to
   report to RSM at 1745 hrs.
      "A" Coy will provide a loading
   party of 1 Offr 1 Sgt 2 Cpls 25 Pts

to report to QM at Station at 1700 hrs

Coys will arrange for an officer to be responsible for seeing that no men of their Coy leave the train without permission.

All water bottles will be filled before leaving Camp.

All officers valises to be returned to Station by 1700 hrs.

O i/c Coys will furnish a certificate to the O/R by 1745 hrs that their lines have been left clean.

SCHALL
Captain & Adjutant

SECRET. VOLUME No. IV

- - - WAR DIARY - - -

of the

2/15th BN. LONDON REGT. (P. W. O. CIVIL SERVICE RIFLES)

for the month of JULY 1918

\* \* \* \* \* \* \* \* \* \* \* \* \* \* \*

IN THE FIELD
4th AUGUST 1918

LIEUT,-COLONEL
COMMANDING 2/15th BN. LONDON REGIMENT.

CONFIDENTIAL

WAR DIARY

of

3/18th Battalion London Regiment.
(P.W.O.) Civil Service Rifles.

1st – 31st July 1916.

Volume IV

Army Form C. 2118.

# WAR DIARY
## *or*
## INTELLIGENCE SUMMARY.

(*Erase heading not required.*)

Instructions regarding War Diaries and Intelligence Summaries are contained in F. S. Regs., Part II. and the Staff Manual respectively. Title pages will be prepared in manuscript.

| Place | Date | Hour | Summary of Events and Information | Remarks and references to Appendices |
|---|---|---|---|---|
| | | | | |

(A8=04) Wt W17771/M2031 759,000 5/17 D. D. & L., London, E.C. **Sch. 52** Forms/C2118/14

Army Form C. 2118.

# WAR DIARY
## or
## INTELLIGENCE SUMMARY.
*(Erase heading not required.)*

Instructions regarding War Diaries and Intelligence Summaries are contained in F. S. Regs., Part II. and the Staff Manual respectively. Title pages will be prepared in manuscript.

| Place | Date | Hour | Summary of Events and Information | Remarks and references to Appendices |
|---|---|---|---|---|
| SHEET 27 & 8 1/20000 Q 17 b 2.9 | 1/7/18 | 1200 | Detrained at AUDRUICQ. Marched off at 3 p.m. to billets at MOULLE. Attached to 90th BDE, 30th DIV. Advance party (transport) regained unit. | P.H. |
| — "— | 2/7/18 | | Cleaning up. One day Gas Course for Coy Commanders & N.C.O's. Baths. | P.H. |
| — "— | 3/7/18 | | Baths. Training. | P.H. |
| — "— | 4/7/18 | | Training. MAJOR A.W. GAZE, M.C., CAPT F.W. LEWIS, M.C. & 2 O/R's to U.K. on leave. | P.H. |
| — "— | 5/7/18 | | Training. 1 O/R's to U.K. on leave. | P.H. |
| — "— | 6/7/18 | | Training. Tactical Exercise without troops. LT. F.H. DUHEAUME & F.W. PHELPS & 2 O/R's to U.K. on leave. CAPT AND REV G.H. WEST. C.F attached for duty. | P.H. |
| — "— | 7/7/18 | | Bn. Church Parade. 1 O/R's on leave to U.K. Orders for move received. | P.H. |
| — "— | 8/7/18 | 0845 | Bn. moved to RENESCURE area. Bn moved to LE NIEPPE arriving at 1240 am & billeted for the night. CAPTS K.A. WILLS & F.W. LEECH & 2 LT. R. D'NEARLY & H.T. MALLETT & 14 on leave to U.K. | App I |
| T.11. a 7.8. | 9/7/18 | 0710 | Bn. left billets and marched via Q.19 central thence ST SYLVESTRE CAPPEL & ECKE. Bn. in corps reserve responsible for manning front of BERTHEN to FENGIS in case of alarm. — COQ DE PAILLE sector | App II P.H. |

# WAR DIARY or INTELLIGENCE SUMMARY

Army Form C. 2118.

| Place | Date | Hour | Summary of Events and Information | Remarks and references to Appendices |
|---|---|---|---|---|
| MAP REF SHEET 27 SE 1/20000 Q.19.b.6.1 | 10/7/18 | | Training. Reconnaissance of defences by Coy Commanders & Officers. LT. F.W. HOUNSELL & 90 Inf Bde H.Q. as Intelligence Officer. 2 O.R's to U.K. on leave. | P.M. |
| - " - | 11/7/18 | | Training. Reconnaissance of defences by Officers. Relief of 8th battalion commences. | P.M. |
| - " - | 12/7/18 | | Practice manning of COQ DE PAILLE defences. Batt Hqrs. Relieved at 12 midnight & arrived at Berthen at 3.30am. Leave with 2/14 LON REGT established at 3.35 am. 3000 returned to Batt and at 11.30am. LT H.H. SIMPSON at 2 P.M. Twenty two staff and Battn Officers. A Coy returned from leave. A Coy relieved for work on BERTHEN LINE. 2 O.R's to U.K. on leave. | P.M. |
| - " - | 13/7/18 | | Inspection of Bde by Army Commander took N.C.O at 10.30 am. 2 O.R's to U.K. on leave. 3 O.R's to PIGEON Course. 2 LT A. CHILDS (21st Middx Regt) joined for duty & posted to A COY. 2LT L.C. LANDER (8th Essex R) joined for duty & Posted to B COY. 2 LT E. JONES (8th Essex R) joined for duty & posted to D COY. | P.M. |
| - " - | 14/7/18 | | Voluntary Church Service. 4 O.R's to U.K. on leave. LT W.S. MURRAY to hospital. 2LT E.N. WHEELER & 1 O/R to L.G. course, LUMBRES. 1 Sgt Nurse to Berkeley home. | P.M. |
| - " - | 15/7/18 | | Training. 2LT W. BUTLER, 2/3 Batt Essex Regt joined for duty & posted to D COY. 4 O.R's on leave to U.K. Enemy plane was seen flying very low over morning - chaffed our horse & shells. 3 O.R's to Rann Rouge course. | P.M. |
| - " - | 16/7/18 | | Training. Draft of 89 O.R's received from base. 4 O.R's on leave to U.K. G.O.C. 30th Inf aux Brigade MAJOR A.W. GAZE M.C. to new Billets of LT.COL. 3 O/R's to Pigeon Course. 2 O.R's to L.G. course MERCK 5GHEM. 2LT F.E. L. MILLER & 3 O.R's to gas course & CORPS. | P.M. |

# WAR DIARY or INTELLIGENCE SUMMARY

Army Form C. 2118.

*(Erase heading not required.)*

| Place | Date | Hour | Summary of Events and Information | Remarks and references to Appendices |
|---|---|---|---|---|
| MAP REF SHEET 27 C.8 1/20,000 Q.19.b.6.1 | 17/7/18 | | Training. 2 O/R's from leave joined the batt. 4 O/R's on leave to U.K. 6 O/R's on A.A.L.G. course. | PM |
| Q.19.b.6.1 | 18/7/18 | | Practice manning of Battle Stations at S.R.10.c.63. Batt. O/R's Relieved at 12 midnight & arrived at Station 4.20a.m. Relieved to Billets at 5.30a.m. Lt. F.W. PHELPS struck off strength on joining M.G. School, GRANTHAM. Auth. A.G.16. 14 July. 4 O/R to U.K. on leave. | 8A |
| -do- | 19/7/18 | | Training. CAPT C. SADLER, 1st Batt Kendals Regt. taken on strength of this unit. Auth. A/9/108/h 309(0) dated 10/7/18. 4 O/R's to U.K. on leave. MAJOR A.C.H. BENKE, M.C. Pres'd't, & CAPT B. PEATFIELD, M.C. Members of F.G.C.M. at 9/6 L.R. H.Q. 19 O/R's joined from base. TEST ORDERS received 11.30. Joined 11.37. Reserve Coy boys at H.Q. 11.43. A Coy at 12.10 a.m. B & D Coys at 11.45 a.m. Batt. estimated to have at 1a.m. | PTO |
| -do- | 20/7/18 | | Training. Strength 11 O/R's joined from Base. LT. COL. A.W. GAZE, M.C., CAPT F.W. LEWIS, M.C. & 1 O/R rejoined from leave. | SK |
| -do- | 21/7/18 | | Voluntary Church Parade. MAJOR A.C.H. BENKE, M.C., CAPT H.T.G. BACK & 2 O/R's on leave to U.K. 2 O/R's from leave rejoined course. | PM |
| -do- | 22/7/18 | | Gas demonstration by the Gas Officer at P.24.a.63. LT. F.H. DU HEAUME, LT. T.N. PEARSON & 3 O/R's from Rifle Course. TEST ORDERS received at 12 noon. Received by all Coys by 12.10 p.m. | BT |
| -do- | 23/7/18 | | Raining – Aircraft demonstration postponed. CAPT. S.C. HALL, LT. T.N. PEARSON & 2 O.R. to U.K. 2/Lt. S.L. MILLER from Gas Course. | 7HBR |

**Army Form C. 2118.**

# WAR DIARY
## or
## INTELLIGENCE SUMMARY.
(Erase heading not required.)

Instructions regarding War Diaries and Intelligence Summaries are contained in F.S. Regs. Part II. and the Staff Manual respectively. Title pages will be prepared in manuscript.

| Place | Date | Hour | Summary of Events and Information | Remarks and references to Appendices |
|---|---|---|---|---|
| Q.10.b.6.1. | 24.7.18. | | Air-craft demonstration. C.O., Coy. Commanders & Advance Parties up to line. Lt. T.H. ARUNDEL, F.W. HOUNSELL, and 2/Lt H.D. SETTLE to U.K. leave. | A.M.B.M. |
| | 25.7.18. | | Batt. relieved 1/7th Royal Scots in support in Right SUBSECTOR of LOCRE SECTOR - left billets 6 p.m.; relief complete about midnight. Adv. parties sent forward to front line. | App III A.M.B.M. |
| | 26.7.18. | | Batt. relieved 18th H.L.I. in line. "A" Coy on R. "C" Coy R. centre. "B" Coy L. centre. "D" Coy L. Relief complete 1.50 a.m. on 27th. | App IV A.M.B.M. |
| | 27.7.18. | | Day normal. 11.30 p.m. barrage put down in connection with raids by 2 Bdes. on left. Hostile barrage put down on our line. Casualties 2 killed, 9 wounded. | A.M.B.M. |
| | 28.7.18. | | In morning 150-200 shells round barn near "A" Coy - 4 killed. Orders received for relief by 2/4th on night 30/31. | A.M.B.M. |
| | 29.7.18 | | Normal. Advance parties of 2/4th arrive. | A.M.B.M. |
| | 30.7.18 | | Batt. relieved by 2/4th. (Took over billets near BOESEPE, with H.Q. at R.8.c.9.5.) | App V A.M.B.M. |
| | 31.7.18 | | Relief complete at 2.0 a.m. S.O.S. sent up on our left. ✓ 2/Lt WATTS rejoined from course. | A.M.B.M. |

Custage Lt. Col.
Coy 2/17th Battalion London Regiment,
(P.W.O.) Civil Service Rifles.

Appendix I

SECRET.                                                Copy No. 11

## 2/15th Battn. London Regiment.

### ORDER NO. LII.

Ref. Map.
HAZEBROUCK 1/100,000.
SHEET 27. 1/40,000.                              7th July, 1918.

1. The 30th Division (less Artillery) will be transferred from the VII Corps to X Corps at midnight 7th/8th July.

2. The 90th Infantry Brigade Group will move by march route from The SERQUES Area to the RENESCURE Area on the 8th July, and thence to the ST. SYLVESTRE CAPPEL - EECKE Area on the 9th July.

3. The Battn. will parade in column of route ready to march off at 8.30 a.m. Head of Column at Cross Roads, Q.18.c.4.8. Order of March: "H.Q" "A" "B" "C" "D" Coys.
   Distances of 100 yds. to be maintained between Companies, and between Companies and transport.

4. The following instructions on march discipline are to be strictly carried out:
   (a) Keep in threes and closed up. No N.C.O. outside the column.
   (b) Hug the right edge of the road.
   (c) Keep in step by platoons. Sing by platoons; salute by platoons.
   (d) Halt for ten minutes at ten minutes to every 'clock hour,' whatever time you start.
   (e) Fall out on the right. Leave all cross roads and road junctions clear.
   (f) All packs off within 30 seconds of order for ten minute halt. Fall in (by whistle) at one minute to the clock hour.
   (g) Keep transport closed up. Only drivers on vehicles. Brakesman and dismounted men in the column, not on the flank. ALL mounted men off horses within 10 seconds of order to halt, girths loosened, poles of transport down.
   (h) Any details marching with the transport, such as storemen, extra cooks, transport helpers, &c. to march as a formed body in rear under an N.C.O.

5. On arrival at X Corps Area on the 9th, the 30th Division will relieve the 41st French Division in Corps Reserve.

6. The 90th Infantry Brigade while in Corps Reserve, will, in case of attack, be prepared on receipt of orders to man the defences of the BERTHEN Line. Instructions (with maps) regarding the occupation of this line by the Brigade in case of alarm will be issued later.

7. The following officers will report to the C.O. at the Battn. Orderly Room at 8.45 a.m., and will proceed by Motor Lorry to reconnoitre the BERTHEN Line, and the approaches to it. Maps will be provided by Bde.H.Q.
   The party will rejoin the Battn. to-morrow evening.
        Capt. H.J.G. BACK.
        Capt. D. PEATFIELD, M.C.
        Lieut. T.H. ARUNDEL.
        Lieut. A. WHITING.

P.T.O.

8.     Administrative Instructions will be issued later.

                                S. C. HALL,
                                   Capt. & Adjutant.

Issued at 5.30 p.m.

Copy No.1 Major BEHKE, M.C.
       2. O.C., "A" Coy.
       3. O.C., "B" Coy.
       4. O.C., "C" Coy.
       5. O.C., "D" Coy.
       6. O.C., "H.Q" Coy.
       7. Q.M.
       8. M.O.
       9. T.O.
      10. R.S.M.
      11. War Diary.
      12. Retained.

Appendix II                                War Diary

BATTALION ORDERS NO. 142 BY Major A. C. H. BENKE, M.C., Commdg.
Monday, 8th July, 1918.

1. ROUTINE.
Reveille 4.0 a.m.   Breakfast 5.0 a.m.   Sick Parade 5.30 a.m.
Lights Out. 9.30 p.m.

Coy. on duty.   "B"                Next.   "C"
Officer of the day.                2nd Lieut. W.J. MURRAY.
Next.                              2nd Lieut. A.L. TAYLOR.

2. MOVE.
Map Ref. HAZEBROUCK 1/100,000 & Sheet 27 - 1/40,000.
The Battn. will move to Billets at Q.19. central to-morrow.
The Battn. will rendezvous at Road Junction (Sheet 27 - 1/40,000)
U.8.b.8.7. (Sheet HAZEBROUCK 1/100,000 at Cross Roads below last
S. in LES SIX RUES on dividing line between squares F. Nos. 3 & 4 )
at 8.20 a.m.  Order of march: "H.Q." "B" "C" "D" "A" Coys: H.Q. "A" &
"B" Coys. will parade at Road Junction T.11.a.7.8. ready to
march off at 7.10 a.m.  "C" & "D" Coys. will proceed to U.8.b.8.7.
independently with baggage wagons which will report to Transport
Officer on arrival at that point.
TRANSPORT.
1 partly loaded baggage wagon will report to each Coy. at 5.30 a.m
to carry officers' valises, blankets, & Cooks' utensils, Officers Mess
H.Q.Coy. will dump cooks' utensils at Q.M.Stores at 6.0 a.m.
and blankets at 5.0 a.m.  H.Q.Officers valises to be at Q.M.Stores by
6.0 a.m.
All men must leave billets with full waterbottles.

3. The following officers will meet Capt. SADLER (A/Brigade Major)
at Bde. H.Q., EBBLINGHEM, at 8.25 a.m., and will proceed to meet
French Officers at ST SYLVESTER CAPPEL and carry out a reconnaissance
of the BECKE - BERTHEN LINE:- Motor Lorry will be provided.
Lieut. F.W. HOUNSELL - H.Q.
Capt. H.J.C. BACK.
Capt. B. PRATFIELD, M.C.
Lieut. A. WHITING.
Lieut. T.H. ARUNDEL.

4. The G.O.C. noticed the following points on the march to-day.
   1. Men unshaven.
   2. Sections very irregular.
   3. Chin-straps - some up and some down.

The Battn. on joining the new Brigade has brought a good
reputation with it, and the C.O. directs that all ranks pay strict
attention to their march discipline, and so uphold this reputation.
Platoon Commanders will be held responsible that the above faults are
rectified.  All chin-straps will be worn down.  O.C., "A" Coy. will
detail an officer to march in rear of Battn. to bring along any men
who may fall out.

S. C. HALL,
Capt. & Adjutant.

App III

SECRET                                              COPY NO. 12

## 2/15th Battalion London Regiment.

## OPERATION ORDER NO. LIII.

Map Refce.                                          25th July, 1918.
    Sheet 27 S.E. (Eastern Half)) — 1/20,000.
    Sheet 28 S.W.                ))

1.     The Battalion will relieve the 17th Battn. R. Scots in Support to-night. H.Q. will be at N.21.a.5.4.

2.     **Parade.**
    Battn. will pass Starting Point at H.Q. at 6 p.m.
    Order of march: "H.Q" "C" "D" "A". 100 yards between Coys.
    Dress: Fighting Order & groundsheets. No blankets or greatcoats will be taken.
    "B" Coy. will proceed direct. A guide will meet them at GADGET CORNER at 7 p.m.

3.     Coys. will take over from like Coys. Details have been arranged by O's. C. Coys. and advance parties. Guides will meet platoons near the area.

4.     East of GODEWAERSVELDE, advance will be by platoons at 300 yards distance.

5.     Coys. will leave dumps in their Coy. areas, of tools, blankets, packs, and officers' surplus kit, etc. One man will be left with each Coy. limber-load of this dump. 4 dixies will be taken up with each Coy., and the rest left on the dump. 1 cook will go up with each Coy.

6.     Details of rations have been arranged with Coys.

7.     Water is very scarce in the Support area, and great economy is necessary to-morrow.

8.     Officers' kits must be cut down to an absolute minimum.

9.     1 limber per Coy. for L.G., and 1 limber for Coy. baggage, rations, etc., will report to Coys. at 5 p.m. Transport will follow in rear of Battn.

10.     Personnel to remain at rear H.Q. will hold themselves in readiness to report to Q.M. at 1 hour's notice, or upon departure of Battn. Lists of such personnel to be rendered to Orderly Room, in duplicate, by 4 p.m.

11.     Completion of Coy. reliefs to be notified to Battn. H.Q.

12.     On arrival, an advance party of 1 Officer per Coy., & 1 N.C.O. per platoon, will be required to go on to the front line to look round. The same officer who went yesterday can go on, but another N.C.O. per platoon must be selected.

                                                            P.T.O.

13.     While in the line, platoon ration states for the following day will be sent down by returning ration convoy at night.

F. H. DU HEAUME,

Lieut. & Acting Adjutant.

Issued at 1 p.m.

Copy No. 1. C.O.
2. O.C., "A" Coy.
3. O.C., "B" Coy.
4. O.C., "C" Coy.
5. O.C., "D" Coy.
6. Int. Officer.
7. Signals.
8. Q.M.
9. T.O.
10. M.O.
11. R.S.M.
12. WAR DIARY.
13. Retained.

Appendix IV

SECRET.   Copy No. .........

2/15th Battn. London Regiment.
OPERATION ORDER NO. 54.

26th July, 1918.

1. The Battalion will relieve the 18th H.L.I. in the Line to-night, with H.Q. at M.27.b.7.3.

2. Coys. will move off independently at 10.30 pm., with intervals between platoons, and will take over from like Coys. in the line. Guides will have reported to Coys.

3. All trench stores in present area will be handed over to the 2/16th Officer with each Coy., and receipts obtained. One copy will be sent to Orderly Room. Lists of stores taken over in forward area will also be sent to Orderly Room.

4. Before moving off, "A" & "C" Coys. will each draw 24 tins of water from Battalion H.Q., and "H.Q" Coy. 20 tins. Parties to report to R.S.M.

5. Two tin boxes of magazines per gun will be taken up the line. The remainder, together with the gun chests, will be dumped at Battn. H.Q.
Statements of Coy. Dumps will be handed in to Orderly Room.

6. On arrival at new area, ration parties will be sent back to Bde. Dump at Sunken Road, and 15 tins of water per Coy.

F. H. DU HEAUME,

Lieut. & Acting Adjutant.

Issued at 5 pm.

Copies to 4 Coys., M.O. & R.S.M.

SECRET.  *Appendix V*  Copy No. .......

## 2/15th Battn. London Regiment.

### OPERATION ORDER NO. 55.

29th July, 1918.

1. The Battalion will be relieved in the Line on the night of 30/31st inst., by the 2/14th L.R., and will move into reserve with H.Q. at R.8.c.9.5.

2. All maps, air photos, information, trench stores, and work in hand will be handed over on relief, and receipts sent to Orderly Room.

3. One officer per Coy., and 1 N.C.O. per platoon and H.Q. Coy. will remain in with the 2/14th for 24 hours.

4. 16 magazines in two tin boxes will be left in the trenches for each L.G. A similar quantity will be taken over from the 2/14th.

5. One guide per platoon and 1 for H.Q. Coy. will meet the 2/14th at 10.45 pm. at M.20.d.1.8., (in the sunken road). The 2/14th will arrive in the following order :-

    2 front line platoons of "A" and "C".
    "   "    "      "      "   "   "  "B".
    3   "    "      "      "   "   "  "D".

followed by remainder of Coys. in above order.

6. Coys. will hand over following numbers of petrol tins as trench stores :-
    "A" - 24.    "B" - 18.    "C" - 24.    "D" - 18.
    "H.Q" - 14.

All other petrol tins will be brought out of line and loaded on Company limbers.

7. 1 Limber per Coy. & H.Q.Coy. will report to Coys. at the ration dump. Gun chests will be in the limbers.

8. Q.M. will send guides to Daylight Post to meet Coys., and will arrange to have hot tea ready for Battn. at billets.

9. On relief, platoons proceed to Bde. Dump and load limbers, and proceed independently. Close up at LANCET FARM, and then Coys. move with platoon intervals.

10. Completion of relief to be notified to Battn. H.Q. by runner in the usual manner.

11. An advance party of 1 Officer, 4 N.C.Os. & 1 runner per Coy. & 1 Offr., & 4 runners per Battn. H.Q. will arrive to-night.

F. H. DU HEAUME,
Lieut. & Acting Adjutant.

Issued at 8 pm.
Copies to 4 Coys., Q.M., M.O., R.S.M. & O.C., 2/14th L.R.

SECRET.                                           VOLUME No._____

W A R   D I A R Y

of the

2/15th Battalion London Regt.,

(P.W.O.) Civil Service Rifles)

for the month of AUGUST, 1918.


IN THE FIELD.                    W. J. Murray    2nd Lt.,
   3rd Sept.,1918.                    for Lieut.-Colonel,
                        Commanding, 2/15th Battalion London Regiment,
                              (P.W.O.) Civil Service Rifles.

Army Form C. 2118.

# WAR DIARY
or
## INTELLIGENCE SUMMARY.
(Erase heading not required.)

Instructions regarding War Diaries and Intelligence Summaries are contained in F. S. Regs., Part II. and the Staff Manual respectively. Title pages will be prepared in manuscript.

| Place | Date | Hour | Summary of Events and Information | Remarks and references to Appendices |
|---|---|---|---|---|
| R 8. c 9. 5. | 1/8/18 | | Training & working parties. | 5794 |
| " | 2/8/18 | | 2/Lt A.P. PITTAM to General Corns X Corps. 2nd Lt C. LANDER & CAS COURSE X CORPS. Having interviewed that N.C.O. visited 6 ST SYLVESTRE CAPPEL AREA | IN |
| Q 19 b 7. | 13/8/18 | | 1 COY moved back to billet near ST SYLVESTRE CAPPEL. Relieved by 9 Km | IN App I |
| " | 4/8/18 | | Afoot Coy Rend hunt at TERGES HEM. The End of parade was ... Lt Col A.W.GATE, D.C. | IN |
| " | 5/8/18 | | Training MAJOR BANKS MC and CAPT BACK from leave MM YATING joined | IN |
| " | 6/8/18 | | Training Lt A WHITING & Lt T THE CLARK to Corp | IN |
| " | 7/8/18 | | Training ... | IN |
| " | 8/8/18 | | ... Lt RC COOK Lt T MARTIN and A W BURCH joined to day ... Lt COL SURTEES T/O O I/C BN RE A W BURCH Corp. CAPT HALL med Lt PEARSON from Camp | IN |
| R 9 a.h. | 9/8/18 | | 10.55 marched 9.30 to Camp 10 1 12.35 M L I AC 12. 10 ... Move in support to the LOCRE HOF. SUGGESTION of the LOCRE & actor 1.7 Ion marched 9 O C 1.7 12 00 for synchro. | IN App I |
| M 2 a.5.4 | 10/8/18 | | Rest in trenches Lt T.H. ARUNDEL and L/C H D SETTLE from Can | |

D. D. & L. London, E.C.
(A8.04) Wt W1727/M2931 750,000 5/17 **Sch. 52** Forms/C2118/14

Army Form C. 2118.

# WAR DIARY
## or
## INTELLIGENCE SUMMARY.
*(Erase heading not required.)*

Instructions regarding War Diaries and Intelligence Summaries are contained in F. S. Regs., Part II. and the Staff Manual respectively. Title pages will be prepared in manuscript.

| Place | Date | Hour | Summary of Events and Information | Remarks and references to Appendices |
|---|---|---|---|---|
| M22 a 5.4 | 11/8/18 | | 2/Lt L C LANDER from Course. Himself Blown twice at TIERDIGHEM at Return. H.M. the KING attended. MAJOR A.E.H BENNIE, M.C. and 2 O/R's attended. | 9/R |
| - " - | 12/8/18 | | 1 O/R wounded by shell fire. Batt to supply two bays and scaffolds in support for R.E working party. 2/Lt H.E KNORTH wounded probably at ARMIERES. | 9/R |
| - " - | 13/8/18 | | Batt in Support. | 9/R |
| - " - | 14/8/18 | | 90' INF BDE took over the LOCRE HOE SUB-SECTION. Batt manned in support 6 O/R to No 1 Sub Area Commandant CAROME CROSSING for duty as Guards/etc. | 9/R |
| - " - | 15/8/18 | | 1 N.C.O + 10 men to 90' MGC DEMONSTRATION PLATOON. LT P.W. HOUNSELL wounded. | 9/R |
| - " - | 16/8/18 | | Orders received that Batt would relieve the 21/ London Regt on the line. Enemy aeroplane brought down in flames. Three our believe to have been brought down by own Guns firing fired on in A.A fiction. One bay on duty with R.E 3 | 9/R App III. |
| M22 a.c.6.9 | 17/8/18 | 3 a.m | Relief complete. 2 O/R's Killed. Enemy artillery very active during night. C.attention over R.E3. | 9/R |
| | 18/8/18 | | Orders received that 4/6 Lon. Regt would relieve Batt evening night 19/8. Batt to move working parties 1 Coy to the Trenches. | 9/R App IV |
| M22 a.5.4 | 19/8/18 | 12.20 a.m | Relief complete. Orders received that Batt would be relieved by 2/4 London Regt working night of 19/8/20. Batt to move into reserve at MOTH FARM. at R.B.C 2.7. working party 151 bays. Relief complete 11.30 p.m | 9/R App V |
| R.B C 27 | 20/8/18 | | Batt in billets. C Coy + Jenny 2/Lt J.L. HUTCHISON + 4 O/R's from Course | 9/R |
| - " - | 21/8/18 | Act 2.5.m | The 9/ Lon. Regt attacked + captured the Port Lentrn on the DRANOUTRE SPUR. (MGC and coys 17.35 a.m to a completion with the 29 INFBDE on the right and the 2/1 BDE Guns second to advance to the 9/ Lon Regt ... On night of 22/23 This Batt wounds in suppt. | 9/R |

D. D. & L., London, E.C. Wt. W1771/M2931 750,000 5/17 **Sch. 52** Forms C2118/14 (A(001)

# WAR DIARY or INTELLIGENCE SUMMARY

Army Form C. 2118.

| Place | Date | Hour | Summary of Events and Information | Remarks and references to Appendices |
|---|---|---|---|---|
| R 8 c 2.7 | 22/8/18 | | 2/Lt L.C. LANDER to Hospital. Pvt. 4725 Tiller W killed at 8.30 p.m. & relieves the 2/14 Battn on the new line of the LOCREHOF SECTOR. Relief complete at 2 a.m. 23rd. Heavy shelling by enemy during relief. CAPT H.J.G. BACK and 1 O/R wounded during relief. | 8th App II |
| 1.22 c 9.9 | 23/8/18 | | Battn in line. Intermittent shelling by enemy during day. WATERFIELD WOOD shelled with gas shells. Work — self, supply party & wiring. Enfilade to work during daylight. Reliefs carried out by KEMMEL. | SH |
| " | 24/8/18 | | 1 a.m. Enemy artillery very active & heavy shelled front and support trenches. Enemy attacked by bombers in what is held but was driven off by our artillery. One prisoner taken 80/R (3rd Regt)(A Coy). 2/Lt E JONES & 2nd O/R killed. 29 O/Rs wounded. Lt WHITTING and 2LT CLARK and 20/R wounded & evacuated to duty. Returned from line. | SH |
| " | 25/8/18 | | Work — Reliefs informed. Area on boundary H.Q.'s shelled by CAPT R.13 W/Lt ANDREW M.C. filled 2/9 and 8 and shells. 3O/R's killed & wounded. One wounded remained 2/LT H R WRIGHT to Hembly Camp, LUMBRES. | SH |
| " | 26/8/18 | | Orders received that Battn would be relieved during the night of 26/27. On completion of relief A, C & D Coys to move into support line at MONT ROUGE and B Coy to remain in SUPPORT LINE. This coy to work on the BLUE LINE under orders of R.E. 3 O/R's killed. Relief Patrol under Lt F H Do NEAUME & Lt LOCREHOF LOCREHOF FARM was sent to endeavor a point at 1.29, 34.03 but was established at M.29 at 20.63 all the fatal salience reply to own lines. Bomber patrol left on night of 26 under "Lt H S MALLETT" 10 MB PARTY and more gone the end of the Rd at N.13 of the same. No reply was established in a strong outpost by M.G.'s line established under this night on top of the same, there were still Robs at 1.35 & 75.70 where it consolidated. Double Sentries were established at approx 17.35 & 9.3. CAPT A A SOSLIN rejoined from leave. | App VII SH |

# WAR DIARY
## or
## INTELLIGENCE SUMMARY.
*(Erase heading not required.)*

Army Form C. 2118.

| Place | Date | Hour | Summary of Events and Information | Remarks and references to Appendices |
|---|---|---|---|---|
| M22 o 4 | 27/8/18 | 12 noon | Relief completed 170TH I/ARM in right of 28/29. Orders received that battn would move into reserve at 170TH I/ARM in night of 28/29. | PM |
| - | 28/8/18 | | Batt in support at MONT ROUGE. Any bomb shells during the morning 1 O/R wounded. Relief completed at 2am 29th owing to bus never at 170TH I/ARIM. LT F.H. DU HEAUME attached A Coy owing the absence of CAPT DEARFIELD on leave. 2 LT W.J. MURRAY reported from Hospital. | App VIII Nil |
| R8c 2.7 | 29/8/18 | | Batt in reserve at 170TH I/ARM. Training. HQ A & D Coy's billeted at STEENAKERE. 2 LT W.P. WEBB & CAPT. B DEARFIELD MC and RLT L. HUTCHISON MC on leave to U.K. | P.M. |
| - | 30/8/18 | | Training C & D Coy's billeted at STEENAKERE. Batt ordered to be ready to move at 1/2 hrs notice owing to movement of enemy. Standby forces 2nd Army. LT IN ARUNDEL & on leave. | SA |
| - | 31/8/18 | | Batt standby. Orders received at 3pm that batt was to proceed to MONT ROUGE. Relief comp. bill at 3 pm. by another unit. batt order took over outpost position in the vicinity of CURRAGH CAMP. 1 an Engd. M16.19. 2LT W. SANGER. | S/B |

AW Gough  
Lt Col  
Cog 7/15th London Regt

S E C R E T.   Appendix I   COPY No. ............

## 2/15th Battalion London Regt.
## OPERATION ORDER No. LVI.

Ref.Map.  
Sheet 27.S.E. (E.& W.Halves.) 1/20,000   3rd August, 1918.

1. The Battalion will be relieved in Reserve to-night by a Battn. of 106th Bde.

2. On relief, Coys. proceed independently, with intervals between platoons, to former quarters near ST. SYLVESTRE CAPPEL (Q.19.b.7.1.)

3. Dress: Full Marching Order — Blankets will be carried on the man.

4. 1 limber per Coy. for Lewis Guns, ½ limber for Coy. baggage, teams for cookers, & 2 limbers & Mess Cart for H.Q.Coy. will report to-night xxxxxxxxx about 10 pm. All L.G. stores & Coy. baggage will be removed to new area.

5. Usual advance parties will proceed and take over same billets as before.

6. Relief of Coys. will be notified to Battn. H.Q. by runner.

F. H. DU HEAUME,  
Lieut. & Acting Adjutant.

Issued at 1.30 pm.

P.T.O.

Copies to

No. 1. C.O.
2. O.C., "A" Coy.
3. O.C., "B" Coy.
4. O.C., "C" Coy.
5. O.C., "D" Coy.
6. O.C., "HQ" Coy.
7. Q.M.
8. T.O.
9. M.O.
10. R.S.M.
11. Signals.
12. War Diary.
13. Retained.

*Appendix II*  *War Diary*

SECRET.                                                          COPY No. ......

2/15th Battalion London Regt.
Order No. LVIII

Map Ref. 27 S.E. & 28 S.W.
1/20,000.                                                        9th August, 1918.

1.      The Battalion will relieve a Battn. of the H.L.I. this evening, at M.22.a.5.4. Coys. will relieve opposite Coys.

2.      Route. Via. BOESCHEPE – LANCET FARM (R.18.a.3.6.) – BENGAL COTTAGES – WESTOUTRE. Order of March: "H.Q" "A" "B" "C" "D"
        Coys. will pass Starting Point at Junction of Road (R.9.b.8.3.) at the following times:

        "H.Q"   9.30 pm.
        "A"     9.35 pm.
        "B"     9.43 pm.
        "C"     9.51 pm.
        "D"     9.59 pm.

        100 yards interval will be maintained between platoons.
        Dress: Full Marching Order.
        1 Guide per platoon & 1 for transport from the H.L.I. will meet the Battalion at WATER TANKS (R.18.a.3.6.).

3.      Transport.
        1 L.G. Limber will be at the disposal of each Coy. for conveyance of xxGxxSxAxAx Lewis Guns, 16 boxes containing L.G. S.A.A. magazines, 4 dixies and 20 petrol cans full of water. Extra dixies from the cookers may be taken at the discretion of Coy. Commanders.
        Officers' valises and surplus L.G. Magazines to be returned to Q.M. Stores per ration limbers.
        Rations.
        Limbers containing rations will be at R.E. Dump at R.2.c.5.7. at 5 pm. 1 Guide to be sent from each Coy. to bring up limbers. Should limbers be prevented from passing R.2.c.5.7., Coys. will provide carrying parties. Field Kitchens & 1 Water Cart will be returned to Q.M. Stores.

4.      Coys. will inform Orderly Room by 6 pm. the number of Shelters taken over from the Sherwood Foresters.

                                                S. C. HALL,
                                                    Capt. & Adjutant.

Issued at 4.30 pm.
Copies to all concerned.

SECRET.                              2/15th Bn. London Regiment.           Appendix III
                                    ORDER NO. LIX

Ref. Maps. Sheet 27.SE. } 1/20,000.                           15th August 1918.
          Sheet 28.SW. }

1. The Battn. will relieve the 2/14th Lon. Regt. on the night of 16/17th August, in the front line of the LOCRE HOF SUBSECTION.

2 (a) **ADVANCE PARTY.** Dress: Fighting Order.
Each Coy. will send an advance party of 1 Officer and 4 N.C.O's. + H.Q. Coy. 1 N.C.O. to report to H.Q. 2/14th Bn. at M.22.d.0.9. at 11.30 pm. tonight. Rations will be taken for 16th inst.

(b) **REAR PARTY.**
2/Lieut. BUTLER will remain in present area for 24 hours and conduct 2/14th representatives over the INTERMEDIATE LINE, and will then proceed to Q.M. Stores.
1 N.C.O. or Senior Soldier from each Coy. + H.Q. will remain in present area for 24 hours.
This party will rejoin Battn. on night of 17/18th.
Cooks will not go into the line. They will be responsible for loading all packs + cooking utensils on to returning ration limbers. They will then proceed to Q.M. Stores.

3. **DISPOSITIONS.**

| | | |
|---|---|---|
| FRONT LINE | RIGHT | "A" COY. |
| | LEFT | "B" " |
| SUPPORT | RIGHT | "C" " |
| | LEFT | "D" " |

Battn. HQ. — SUNKEN ROAD.
Coys. will take over Coy. HQ's. as under:—
"A" COY — "A" COY.    "B" COY. — "D" COY.
"C"  "  — "B"  "      "D"  "  — "C"  "

Order of Relief of Platoons is as follows:—
No 1. platoon 2/15th relieves No 3 platoon 2/14th.
     2      -        -        4     -      -
     3      -        -        1     -      -
     4      -        -        8     -      -
     5      -        -       15     -      -
     6      -        -       10     -      -
     7      -        -       13     -      -
     8      -        -       11     -      -
     9      -        -        5     -      -
    10      -        -        6     -      -
    11      -        -        7     -      -
    12      -        -        2     -      -
    13      -        -        9     -      -
    14      -        -       16     -      -
    15      -        -       14     -      -
    16      -        -       12     -      -

P.T.O.

(2)

*(margin note: All Officers)*

### 4. GUIDES.

1 Guide per platoon, 1 per Coy. HQ, & 1 for Battn. HQ. from 2/14th Battn. will report to respective Coys. at 12 midnight.

Coys. will move off at 12.30 a.m. in the following order:—
"A" Coy followed by "C" Coy. by night tracks.
"B"   "    "    "D"  "    main C.T.

H.Q. Coy will move at 10 pm.

### 5. RATIONS.

Rations will be issued before leaving present area, & petrol tins of water carried.

QM. will arrange for Tommy's cookers to be issued with rations. All men must leave with water bottles full.

From the night of 17/18th., "C" COY. will provide carrying party to carry "A" Coy's. rations from Dump to "A" Coy's HQ., and "D" Coy. to carry "B" Coy's. rations to No. 6. platoon HQ.

### 6. COMMUNICATIONS

One runner per Coy. will report to Bn. HQ. at M.22.d.0.9. tonight, & will be relieved by H.Q. Coy.

### 7. TRENCH STORES.

Copy of all stores will be taken over by platoons. Copy of receipts will be sent to Battn. O.Room.

Trench Stores in present area will be handed over by platoons to 2/14th Lond.R. Receipts to be forwarded to Battn. O.Room.

### 8. GAS.

Cpl. HART will be responsible for handing over all gas appliances at Battn. HQ.    Sgt. FUNSTON will take over all gas appliances at 2/14th Battn. HQ.

### 9. RELIEF.

Coy. Commanders will report by runner to Battn. HQ. when relief is complete by using their surname.

### 10. MEDICAL.

The R.A.P. is at M.22.b.8.0.

### 11. DUMPS.

The Dumps situated at M.29.a.7.4. and M.28.a.8.5. are on no account to be touched without permission being first obtained from Battn. HQ.

"B" & "A" Coys. respectively will be held responsible for above dumps.

S.C. HALL,
Capt. & Adjutant.

Issued to Coys., H.Q., Rear HQ.

## Defence Scheme.
### 2/15th London Regiment.
### Centre Support - Locre Sector.

Ref. Map. Sheet 28 ypres.
Locre Sketch Map Opere.

1. **Boundaries.**
   (a) **Right Boundary.** Cross roads, M.21.d.5.1. - Road Junction M.21.d.9.5. - N.E. corner Locre convent grounds.
   (b) **Left Boundary.** M.29.l... - M.22.d.0.0. - M.22.b.0.70 - M.22.b.70.65.

2. **Headquarters.**
   - Bde. H.Q. - M.27.a.5.5.
   - Bn. HQ. - M.22.a.5.4.

3. **Role.**
   The Role of the Support Battalion is two fold.
   (a) To hold the Intermediate or Red line in case of a general attack.
   (b) To restore the situation in the Blue line in case of a local attack.

4. The Intermediate Line runs along the S.E. slopes of MONT ROUGE. There is a second line on the N.W. slopes of MONT ROUGE intended as a jumping off place for counter-attacks. This is in a very poor condition.

5. **Allocation of Duties.**
   - Intermediate Line garrison - One Coy.
   - Counter attack Companies - The remainder.

6. **Dispositions** of Garrison Company, as shown on Sketch Map attached.

7. **Action in case of Attack.**
   (a) On S.O.S. going up, Companies will 'stand to'. Garrison Company will push forward a section to position in or near the line to observe and report on progress of action.
   (b) In the event of a raid or local attack.
   As above. If it is quite certain that the attack is only a local one, all four companies are liable to be called on for counter-attack.
   (c) General Attack
   (i) Garrison Company will act as in (a). It will not move forward to the line without orders from Bn. H.Q. but will keep their men in readiness under shelter.
   (ii) Counter attack Companies will remain in present positions and await orders.

P.T.O.

(2)

8. Two Companies are employed nightly for work under the C.R.E.

A.C. Hall
Capt. & Adjutant,
2/15th Battn. London Regiment
(P.W.O.) Civil Service Rifles.

16th Aug. 1918.

## REPORT ON NEW POSITIONS IN LOCREHOF SECTOR.

The line of resistance and the sentry line are as shown on the attached sketch map.

1. The line is held by three Companies, providing a front line of posts, with the balance of the companies holding the line of resistance.

Three platoons are in reserve, one at M.29.a.9.1. and two in the neighbourhood of PROSE FARM. Owing to continual shelling one of these platoons has been moved to the CHATEAU ROAD.

2. LINE OF RESISTANCE. consists of a trench line dug to an average depth of 4' 6" - 5' 0". It is not yet continuous.

Right Company. This line is the least continuous, as it covers a portion taken over from the Right Brigade.

Centre Company. Trench is continuous on the left, but has about six bays on the right still to be joined up.

Left Company. Trench commences 20 yards from the Centre Company and is continuous as far as the Road Fork (M.29.c.9.6.) The line continues then N.E. along the sunken road to point of junction with the Left Brigade. A trench is being dug in a N. direction along the LOCRE-DRANOUTRE ROAD as a flank defence to the platoon N.E. of the Road.

Left Support Platoon. This trench runs from the apex of ANGLE TRENCH in a S.W. direction to within 15 yards of the DRANOUTRE Road. This trench is being continued to connect up with the Left Company.

WIRE.

Right Company. There is a thin fence in front of this Company, which is being strengthened. The posts are being protected with by concertina wire.

Centre Company. The wire in front of this Company was mostly destroyed during the bombardment on the morning of the 23rd. It is being repaired.

Left Company. There is now a fair apron fence in front of this Company as far as and including the DRANOUTRE Road. There was no wire E. of the Road. This is under construction.

LIAISON.

Liaison with the Right Brigade was weak, but proper touch was established last night with that Brigade's front line and the Support Platoon in MOWBRAY WOOD.

On the left liaison is maintained by patrols both by the Front Line Company and the Supporting Platoon, but the Left Brigade's right post is not near enough to their boundary.

GENERAL. The field of fire from the line of resistance is, in the main, good, but I think the right of the line requires throwing forward from 50 to 100 yards, but my strength does not permit of the work being done. Work has been interfered with by bombardment, and the strengthening of the wire requires first attention.

P.T.O.

ENEMY. No definite locations have been obtained, but he has M. G's. in LOCREHOF FARM and has established a post at about 29.d.0.4, but was ejected from it by Rifle Grenades. He has also a M.G. in the neighbourhood of RUMBOLD FARM.

Lt.-Colonel
Comdg. 2/15th Battalion London Regiment
(P.W.O.) Civil Service Rifles.

25th August, 1918.

2/15th LONDON REGT.    Appendix IV

SECRET.    ORDER NO. LX

17th Aug. 1918

Map. Refce.
  Sheet 27 } 1/20,000
       28 }

1. The Battn. will be relieved in the line by the 2/16th LOND. R. on the night of the 18/19th August.

2. On relief, the Battn. will move into Support of the LOCRE HOF Subsection, and Coys. will re-occupy their previous areas.

3. On relief, B Company will take over the duties of Garrison Company.

4. Coys. will bring out of the line all articles of Regtl. and Coy. equipment which they brought in.

5. Q.M. will arrange for dixies and one water cart to be brought up with rations on the night of the 18th inst. Coy. Cooks and Storemen who have been sent down to Rear Details will come up with the rations and will be responsible for guarding their Coy's. rations until collected by Coys. in the morning.

6. O's. C. Coys. will send one guide per Platoon and one per Coy., to be at ~~the following points by~~
  ~~A + C Coys.~~       D. Coy at 9 p.m.
  ~~B + D Coy~~ + Battn. HQ. — A B & C , 9.30 p.m.
  HQ. will undertake the guiding of the relieving Coys. to these points.

7. TRENCH STORES.

Trench Stores, maps, particulars of work in progress and proposed, and aerial photographs will be handed over on relief. Receipts to be sent to Orderly Room by 10. a.m. on the 19th inst. Sgt. Funston will hand over all Gas appliances at Batt. H.Q.

SECRET.  Appendix V  COPY No.

## 2/15th Battalion London Regiment.

### ORDER NO. LXI.

Map Ref.
SHEET 27 - 1/20,000.                                    19th August, 1918.

Battalion will be relieved by 2/14th London Regt. to-night, and will move into Reserve at MOTH FARM. 2/14th London R. is expected to arrive about 11.15 pm.

Coys. will move off independently on relief.

Advance parties of 1 N.C.O. per platoon will report to LT. F. H. DU HEAUME at 5 pm., at R.8.c.8.5.

Trench Stores and Gas Appliances will be handed over and receipts forwarded to Battalion Orderly Room by 10 am. on the 20th inst.

### TRANSPORT.

1½ limbers will report to each Coy., and 1 limber to H.Q. at 10.30 pm., to convey cooking utensils, L.Guns, Magazines and Petrol tins to new area. Medical cart will report to R.A.P.

### RATIONS.

Q.M. will arrange for cooks to proceed in advance and prepare hot tea for troops on arrival. For this purpose 1 Field Kitchen will be used by "HQ"& "A" Coys., 1 Field Kitchen by "D" & "B" Coys., and 1 by "C" Coy.

S. C. HALL,
Capt. & Adjutant.

Copies to Coys., H.Q., & Rear.

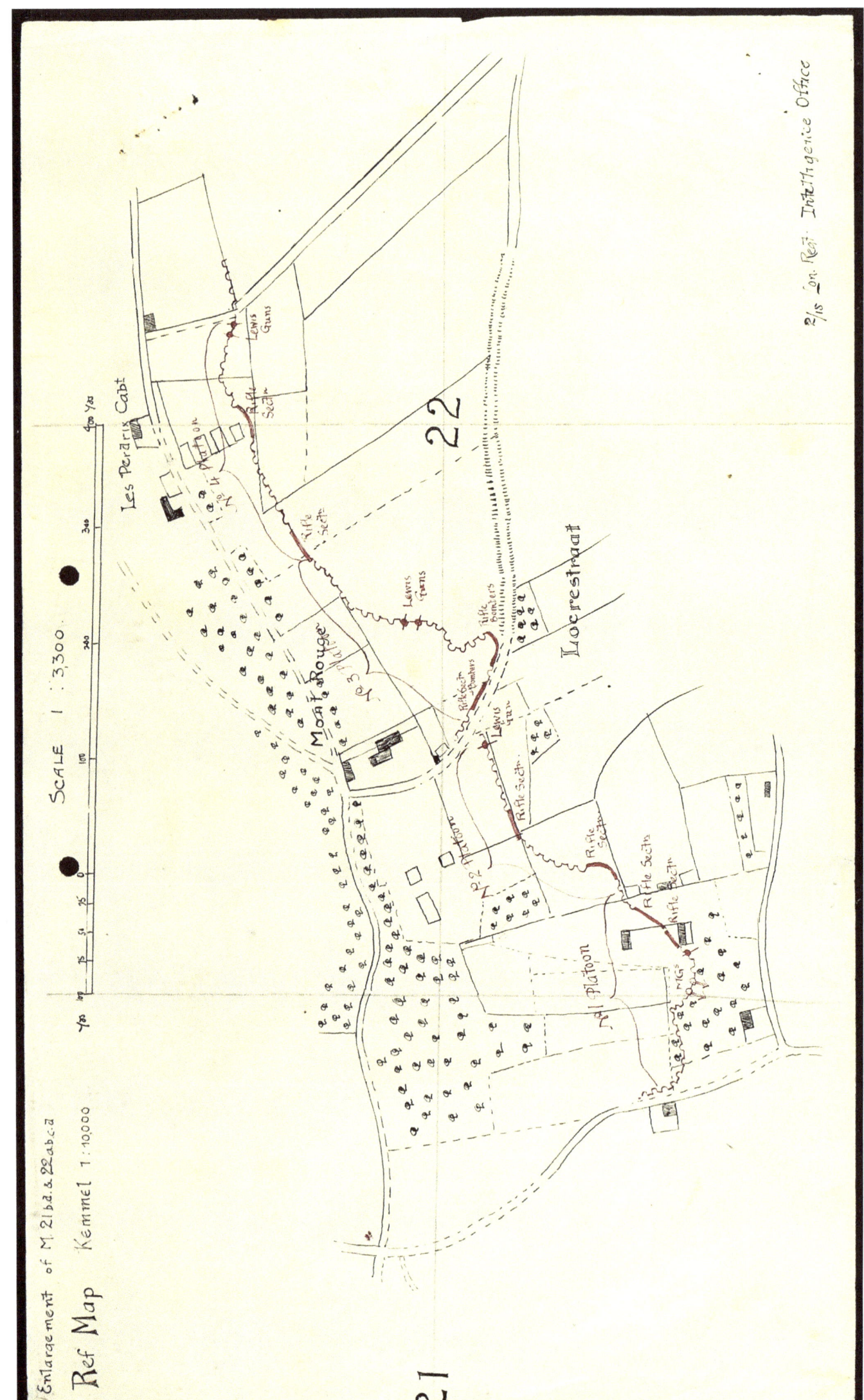

SECRET.                                                    Copy No. 10

## 2/15th Battn. London Regiment.
## ORDER NO. LXII.

21st Aug., 1918.

Map Ref.
SHEET 27 1/20,000
& KEMMEL 1/10,000

1. The Battn. will relieve the 2/14th London Regt. to-morrow night in the new line secured on the 21st inst.
DRESS: Fighting Order, Cardigans wrapped in ground sheets and strapped on belts. One day's rations will be carried plus iron ration.

2. The Battn. will move off in the following order : "C", "A", "D" "B" & "H.Q." Coys. will pass the Starting Point ( R.9.b.8.3.) where Route 4 enters BOESCHEPE at the following times.

    "C"  8.50
    "A"  8.52       Route via LANCHT FARM & BENGAL COTTAGES.
    "D"  9.0
    "B"  9.2
    H.Q. 9.4.

3. ROUTE INTO TRENCHES.
    "C" and "B" to the left via SUNKEN ROAD and Old Battn. H.Q.
    "A" and "D" to the right via QUARRIES.

4. DISPOSITIONS.
    The front line will be held by 3 Companies.
    Coys. will take over as under :
    "A" Coy. right relieves "A" Coy. 2/14th Lond. Regt.
    "D" Coy. Centre     "    "B" "         do.
    "C" Coy. left       "    "C" "         do.
"B" Coy. will be in Reserve with Hd. Qrs. at M.29.d.7.2. This Coy. will be prepared to furnish two Platoons to connect up with Right Battalion Left Brigade.
    Battn. Head Qrs. will be at DAY M.22.d.9.9. NIGHT M.28.d.9.2.

5. (a) ADVANCE PARTIES.
    1 Officer and 1 N.C.O. per Platoon and 1 N.C.O. for Hd. Qrs. Coy. will go up to-night and take over. Above party will report to the 2/14th London Regt.-L.R. H.Q. who will direct them to their respective areas.

   (b) REAR PARTIES.
    All Cooks above two per Coy. will remain behind until all surplus stores left in present billets have been sent to the Q.M. Stores. They will then report to Q.M.

6. TRANSPORT.
    Two limbers per Coy. and one for Battn. Hd. Qrs. and Medical Cart will report to Coys. etc. at 7. p.m. Limbers will accompany Companies. Coys. Q.M.S's will go with limbers and ensure touch is not lost with Coys.
    The T.O. will arrange for returning limbers to report to present Coy. and H.Q. billets and collect any stores left behind and return same to Q.M. Stores. Field Kitchens will be taken to Transport Lines.
    Officers' Riders will report at 8 p.m.

P.T.O.

7. Two Cooks per Coy. will proceed with Battn. and remain in the Quarries in Support Area and take over the SAWYER STOVES. They will [...] to make tea for "A" "B" "C" & "D" Coys. and have same ready at 9.30 P.M. each night. For this purpose the Q.M. will arrange for one day's Tea, Sugar and Milk allowance to be left with Cooks.

8. M-GUNS. LEWIS GUNS.

Three boxes of L.G. S.A.A. in magazines per gun will be taken up to the line. Two boxes per gun will be taken into the trenches and the third box dumped at the quarries under Coy. arrangements.

9. AMMUNITION.

The Q.M. will arrange for 100 bandoliers of S.A.A. to be placed in each Coy. limber. This will be distributed to men on arriving at the quarries. Coys. will arrange for this extra ammunition to be stored in a suitable place on arriving in the trenches. This ammunition will constitute a Coy. Reserve.

10. DUMPS.

Dumps of ammunition and stores have been formed at the following places :-

  No. 1 Dump   M.23.d.6.8.
  No. 2 Dump   M.23.b.6.2.
  No. 3 Dump   M.29.a.7.5.
  No. 4 Dump   M.29.a.8.5.
  No. 5 Dump   M.23.d.9.4.

Dumps Nos. 3 & 4 are to be kept separate.
The Reserve Coy. will take over these dumps and report present contents to O.R. as soon as possible.

11. R.A.P. will be established at M.22.b.8.0. Relay Posts will be established at ROSE FARM.

"A" and "B" Coys. will each detail one man to report to the R.A.P. for instruction in Stretcher Bearing. They will live with and be rationed by the R.A.P.

Sanitary Men will remain with Coy. H.Qrs. whilst in the trenches.

12. GAS.

Sgt. FUNSTON will arrange to take over all gas appliances. One Box of Box Respirators will be dumped at Battn. Hq. Qrs. at M.22.d.0.9. Coys. will arrange for any man with defective Box Respirator to report to Sgt. Funston and have same changed.

13. RATIONS & WATER.

All Coys. will arrange to carry their own rations and petrol cans from the limbers. All empty petrol tins must be returned to the limbers. The R.S.M. will check the numbers returned by each Coy. and will arrange for a corresponding number to be issued on the following evening. Brakesmen behind each limber will be held responsible for seeing that no petrol tins fall off limbers and that correct numbers are handed over to Water Duty Men. One Water Cart will be brought up each day and left with Coy. Cooks.

14. COMMUNICATIONS.

The Signalling Officer will arrange to take over all communications.

              P.T.O.

RUNNERS.   One Runner per Coy. will report to Battn.
Head Qrs. at 8 p.m. to-night.  They will live with and be rationed
by Hd. Qrs. Coy. whilst in the trenches.

15.   Officers will arrange to take up as little as possible as
accommodation, so far as is known, is very ~~little.~~ limited.

16.   Completion of reliefs will be reported by Runner in the usual
way to Battn. Head Qrs.


                                    S. C. H A L L

                                              Capt. & Adjt.

Issued to all Coys.

SECRET.                Appendix VII                    WAR DIARY
           2/15th BATTN. LONDON REGIMENT.
           OPERATION ORDER NO. LXIII.

                                            25th Aug., 1918.

   The Battn. will be relieved by the 2/16th London Regiment
to-morrow night (26th/27th/.

   Guides will probably not be required.

   On relief "A", "D" & "C" Coys. will re-occupy old positions
in support area and "B" Coy. will relieve the 2/16th L.R. in
support - two platoons on the left in sunken road at M.22.b. and
two platoons on the right in Sunken Road M. 28.a.

   All equipment taken into the line will be brought out.
Receipts for trench stores handed over to bbe forwarded to Orderly
Room by 12 noon, 27th.

*"C" Coy will occupy "B"*                        S. C. HALL
*Coys area*                                      Capt. & Adjt.

Appendix VII   WAR DIARY

BATTALION ORDERS BY LT.-COL. A.W.GAZE, M.C. Cmmdg.

TUESDAY 27th AUGUST, 1918.

1. Stand to 4.30 a.m. to 5.30 a.m.     and   8.30 p.m. to 9.30 p.m.

2. The Battalion will be relieved to-morrow night by the 2/14th London Regiment and will move into Reserve at MOTH FARM.
   Companies will move off independently on relief.
   Companies will occupy previous billets.
   Advance Parties of 1 Officer and 4 N.C.O's per Coy. will report to the 2/14th London Regiment to-morrow afternoon to take over.
   The Q.M. will arrange for Field Kitchens and Rations to be sent to Billets at Moth Farm.
   Company Cooks will proceed in advance and prepare tea for the troops.
   Trench Stores and Gas Appliances will be handed over and receipts forwarded to Battalion Orderly Room by 10 a.m. on the 29th.

TRANSPORT
   The Transport Officer will arrange for 1½ limbers per Coy. and 1 for Hd. Qrs. Coy. to report at 10 p.m. for conveying Lewis Guns, L.G. Magazines, Cooking Utensils and Petrol Tins. Medical Cart will report to R.A.P.     Officers' Riders to report at 10.30 p.m.

3. Lieut. F.H.DU HEAUME assumes command of "A" Company during the absence of Captain B. PEATFIELD, M.C. on leave.
   Captain R.B.W.G. ANDREW, M.C. takes over command of "D" Coy. from to-day on returning from leave and Lieut. T.H.ARUNDEL will return to "B" Company.

S. C. HALL
Capt. & Adjutant.

Issued to all concerned.

Index..........................

# SUBJECT.

2/15th London Regt

90/30

| No. | Contents. | Date. |
|---|---|---|
| | September 1918. | |

SECRET

WAR DIARY
of
2/15th Battn London Regt
for
September 1918.

J. C. Hall
Capt. & Adj
t/o/c 2/15 London Regt

Army Form C. 2118.

# WAR DIARY
## or
## INTELLIGENCE SUMMARY.
*(Erase heading not required.)*

Instructions regarding War Diaries and Intelligence Summaries are contained in F. S. Regs., Part II. and the Staff Manual respectively. Title pages will be prepared in manuscript.

| Place | Date | Hour | Summary of Events and Information | Remarks and references to Appendices |
|---|---|---|---|---|
| SHEET 28. SW 1/20000 | | | | |
| M.6.b.1.9 | 1/9/18 | | Information received that enemy had evacuated MONT KEMMEL and was retiring to the MESSINES RIDGE. 90th BDE in DIV RESERVE. Batt to provide working parties on the LOCRE-DRANOUTRE ROAD. Orders afterwards cancelled. 90th BDE to be prepared to relieve the 21st BDE. 2nd LT R.V. MOORE joined for duty & posted to D COY. | App. I |
| | 2/9/18 | | Orders received that 90th BDE would relieve the 21st BDE & the Batt. to relieve the 1/23rd LON REGT in support at DONEGAL FARM. Batt moved off at 2 p.m. via LOCRE & DRANOUTRE. LON REGT had, in the meantime, moved forward into the line and later orders were received that the Batt would remain at DONEGAL FARM. 2/14 LON REGT to provide covering guard. | App. I |
| N.31.d. | 3/9/18 | | Batt received orders to hold one company in readiness to support the 2/14 LON REGT at WULVERGHEM. At 5.10 a.m. D COY moved forward to N.33.a.7.5. Later orders received to relieve the 2/14 LON REGT at dusk. Batt moved off at 8 p.m. 2nd LT A.W. BURCH rejoined Batt from Hospital. | App. I |

# WAR DIARY
## or
## INTELLIGENCE SUMMARY.
*(Erase heading not required.)*

Army Form C. 2118.

| Place | Date | Hour | Summary of Events and Information | Remarks and references to Appendices |
|---|---|---|---|---|
| N.33.a.7.5 | 4/9/18 | 2 a.m | Relief completed. DISPOSITION of Coys. B Coy on the right about T.6 central. D Coy on the left about N.36 central. C Coy in support in rear. B Coy at WULVERGHEM and 3 platoons A Coy at N.35.d and 1 platoon in reserve at 13.00. N.2.a. Casualties - 2nd LT E.J. MARTIN killed, CAPT R.B.W.G. ANDREW M.C. wounded in action & remained at duty. 4 O/R's killed. 3 O/R's wounded. 13 O/R's wounded in action. During the afternoon C Coy's position heavily shelled & C Coy moved forward to T.6.c. Relieving in reserve 3 pnd A Coy at dusk. CAPT K.A. WILLS M.C. to hospital. During the night patrols were pushed forward & posts established at N.36.b & D and T.6.b. | 9th |
| N.33.a.7.5 | 5/9/18 | | In the line. Casualties 2nd LT E.W. WATTS wounded. 1 O/R killed 4 O/R's wounded. Wires received from G.O.C. 13 Div congratulating 7 Batt. on excellent progress made. Information received from 36 Div. through 13 Bde that enemy were believed to be retiring. Batt. was to move 100 daylight patrols forward | |

Army Form C. 2118.

# WAR DIARY
## or
## INTELLIGENCE SUMMARY.
(Erase heading not required.)

| Place | Date | Hour | Summary of Events and Information | Remarks and references to Appendices |
|---|---|---|---|---|
| | | | and establish posts on MESSINES RIDGE. Forward coys reported enemy's M.G's and snipers very active & further move cancelled. Orders received that Batt would be relieved by 2/6 LON REGT at dusk. | 7xx. |
| N31D | 6/9/18 | 7 a.m. | Relief completed 7 a.m. Batt moved back into "support" reserve at DONEGAL FARM | |
| " " | 7/9/18 | | At DONEGAL FARM 2nd LT A.L. TAYLOR returned from leave. 2nd LT W.P. WEBB from GAS COURSE. Orders received that 90th BDE would be relieved by the 89th BDE on night of 8/9th & moved to support coys about M 26, 29, 34 & 35. Batt to remain at DONEGAL FARM | 2xx. |
| " " | 8/9/18 | | PTE BROMPTON, B COY reported wounded W/H. PTE CLEAVER, B COY who remained with the Resumption regiment. Orders received that 90th BDE would be relieved by the 21st BDE on the night of 9/10th & move into DIV. RESERVE. | 8xx. |
| " " | 9/9/18 | | Batt moved back to MONT VIDAIGNE & took over area occupied by 1/6th C.O. attended Conference at Bde. | 9xx 9x. |

CHESHIRES.

# WAR DIARY or INTELLIGENCE SUMMARY

Army Form C. 2118.

| Place | Date | Hour | Summary of Events and Information | Remarks and references to Appendices |
|---|---|---|---|---|
| M.&L.O. B.N. 10/9/18 | | Evening | 2nd Lts W IBUTLER & A PITTAM from Lewis Gun School Course | 974 |
| | 11/9/18 | | 2nd Lt A CHILDS & E N WHEELER to base | |
| | 12/9/18 | | Better July. Two companies provided working parties MONT NOIR CHATEAU M19 d 3505. Wet weather consequently interfered with training. | 974 |
| | 12/9/18 | | The Corps Commander presented MM ribbons to the undermentioned at the Quarries, MONT NOIR. Boots provided on stage for parade. Recipients :- Sgts TICKLE, KELLY & WARD, L/Cpl HULL, Ptes SHEPHARD & AYRIES. 2nd Lt W J MURRAY to base report. 2nd Lt E C HEPWORTH reported from casualty for Medical Board. 2nd Lt Porteous to C Coy. | 974 |
| | 13/9/18 | | A & D Coys provided working parties at WESTOUTRE. B & C Coys training. During the morning & in the afternoon B Coy bathed at ranch from M15 d y 2 and C Coy bathed both under Bath arrangements. | 974 |
| | 14/9/18 | | Better July. A & D Coys at work in WESTOUTRE. B & C Coys working at MONT NOIR CHATEAU. 2nd Lt G L BONNER to base from course | |

# WAR DIARY
## or
## INTELLIGENCE SUMMARY.
(Erase heading not required.)

Army Form C. 2118.

| Place | Date | Hour | Summary of Events and Information | Remarks and references to Appendices |
|---|---|---|---|---|
| Mâle S.L. | 14/9/18 | | X" CORPS   2 LT J.L. HUTCHISON, M.C. from leave. | 84 |
| " | 15/9/18 | | A & D COYS continued work in the WESTOUTRE   H.Q. B & C COYS attended | |
| | | | Church parade at 9.30 a.m. & carried out training for line for the afternoon. | 84 |
| | | | D. COY trades at Leave M.T. & Y.Z. into A COY | |
| | | | Rec. Bat. baths & recreation arrangements.   MAJOR A.C.H. BENKE | |
| | | | M.C. from Batt. from Reception Camp (30. B.M.) | |
| | 16/9/18 | | Batt. on duty. Two cups at WESTOUTRE and one at MONT NOIR CHATEAU | |
| | | | A & D COYS moved to MONT NOIR   No 633713 PTE JOSLIN, L.M. | |
| | | | tried by F.G.C.M.   CAPT S.C. HALL prosecutor.   CAPT B.W.G. | |
| | | | ANDREW, M.C. from leave.   CAPT B. PEATFIELD, M.S. from | 84 |
| | | | leave.   2" LT H. WRIGHT from leave.   2" LT H. MALLETT, S. | |
| | | | COY on arrest on command.   LT W. PEARSON to D COY on arrest | |
| | | | in command.   2" LT H. WRIGHT to TRANSPORT | |
| | 17/9/18 | | B & C COYS found working parties at WESTOUTRE   A & D COYS training | |
| | | | 2" LT V.S. BURT to hospital   CAPT B.W.G. ANDREW, M.C. to Leave Gen | 84 |
| | | | Course STAPLES.   LT COL A.W. GAZE, M.C. to PARIS on leave. | |
| | | | crossover command of Batt. | |
| | | | MAJOR A.C.H. BENKE, M.C. | |

# WAR DIARY or INTELLIGENCE SUMMARY

Army Form C. 2118.

(Erase heading not required.)

| Place | Date | Hour | Summary of Events and Information | Remarks and references to Appendices |
|---|---|---|---|---|
| M.21.a.5.1. | 18/9/18 | | A, B & D Coys provided working parties. C Coy training. Reconnaissance of WULVERGHEM SECTOR by C.O. & Coy Cmdrs. Orders received that Batt. would take over from Suffolks & Devon Batts. of 109. B.D.E. 2nd Lt F.W. WATTS & Lt F.H. DUMBADZE to be S/S of Capt Cook 16.2.18. To U/K 10-9-18. | ptd. |
| — | 19/9/18 | | 2 hrs training during the morning. Batt. relieved 1st & 2nd R.I.R. in NEUVE EGLISE SECTOR and remained in support. Relief complete 11.45 p.m. | App III ptd. ptd. |
| T.10.b.6.7 | 20/9/18 | | In support. Enemy shelling. Lt F.W. HOUNSELL struck off strength. Enemy shelled our outposts by 'C' Coy. No casualties. Batt. G.R.O. N. 869. | ptd. |
| — | 21/9/18 | | Relief of guard. Leave to U.K. reopened at 8 O/Rs per day. | ptd. |
| — | 22/9/18 | | 2 working parties, 75 O/Rs. A. 25 O/Rs. B. 13 and 75 O/Rs. C. 25 O/Rs. D. Coy furnished for work for forward bath. Casualties 2 O/Rs killed 2 O/Rs wounded. 2nd Lt. P. WEBB to hospital. Orders received to be prepared to relief Batt. of 1BDE on night of 23/24 at T.6.b.7.1. Preliminary reconnaissance made | ptd. App IV |

# WAR DIARY
## or
## INTELLIGENCE SUMMARY.
*(Erase heading not required.)*

Army Form C. 2118.

| Place | Date | Hour | Summary of Events and Information | Remarks and references to Appendices |
|---|---|---|---|---|
| T.O.b 6.7 | 23/9/18 | | Orders to move postponed. 2ⁿᵈ LT MOORE temporarily attached to A Coy. | 24 |
| | | | CAPT R.B.W.G. ANDREW awarded BAR to M.C. LT A. WHITING M.C. | |
| | 24/9/18 | | Orders to relieve 7/8 R.I.F. 8.G. 13.B.15 on night 26/27 received. Preliminary discussion of forthcoming operations discussed at C.O's meeting. CAPT F.H. DU HEAUME to command C. Coy temporarily. 2ⁿᵈ LT H.J. MALLETT to Rest leave to FRANCE. 2ⁿᵈ LT A.L. TAYLOR to BASE for several source. 2ⁿᵈ LT R.C. COOKE to hospital. | |
| | | | received CAPT K.A. WILLS M.C. transferred to U.K. 18/9/18. | |
| | 25/9/18 | | Reconnaissance of lines to be taken over from the 7/8 R.I.F. | 22 |
| | 26/9/18 | | Batt. moved at 8 p.m. to relieve 7/8 Batt. Royal Irish Fusiliers in line. Batt. H.Q. at T.6.c.7.1. Relief completed 11:30 p.m. A & B Coys in line from STINKING Redoubt & both occupied Rest portion of the WULVERGHEM MESSINES RD. FARM - GABION FARM RD. (excl) to the WULVERGHEM MESSINES RD. (incl). D Coy in support and D Coy in reserve at NEUVE EGLISE | OPP. V. |
| | | | DISPOSITION - FORWARD COYS on the right A Coy. Left, B Coy. | |
| | | | LT COL A.W. GAZE from PARIS LEAVE | |
| T.6.7.1 | 27/9/18 | | Orders received for forthcoming operations. CAPT R.B.W.G. ANDREW M.C. from leave | |

Army Form C. 2118.

# WAR DIARY
## or
## INTELLIGENCE SUMMARY.
(Erase heading not required.)

| Place | Date | Hour | Summary of Events and Information | Remarks and references to Appendices |
|---|---|---|---|---|
| T6c7.1 | | | 2nd Lt. R.C. Cooke from hospital. | |
| " | 28/9/18 | | Information received pointing to the probability of the enemy withdrawing. Batt. received orders to advance in conjunction with Batt. on right & left x capture MESSINES. At 5.30 a.m. A & C Coys pushed forward fighting patrols - object being to capture BIG BULL COTTAGE x secure the line from U.1.b.35.40 to U.1.d.90.60. At 6.45 situation. | App VI |
| | | | Forward fighting patrols - object being to capture BIG BULL COTTAGE x secure the line from U.1.b.35.40 to U.1.d.90.60. At 6.45 situation received at Batt. H.Qrs. At 3 a.m. barrage opened & attack by right batt. on our line was pushed forward to the ST IS & NE BECK. General advance was ordered 6 p.m. | |
| | | | Advance guards were sent forward & A Coy reached MESSINES but had to withdraw owing to battalion on flank not being up. A Coy established H.Qrs at HOSPICE MILL. C Coy's line was echelon back 100 x to Rup. touch with A Coy & right batt. At 9.30 p.m. our line was approx. HOSPICE MILL, SNIPERS HOUSE & U.2.c.9.5.3a. B Coy were ordered to Rup close touch with forward | App III |

Army Form C. 2118.

# WAR DIARY
## or
## INTELLIGENCE SUMMARY.
*(Erase heading not required.)*

Instructions regarding War Diaries and Intelligence Summaries are contained in F. S. Regs., Part II. and the Staff Manual respectively. Title pages will be prepared in manuscript.

| Place | Date | Hour | Summary of Events and Information | Remarks and references to Appendices |
|---|---|---|---|---|
| | 29/9/18 | | Coys. D Coy moved up to the front line. Verbal instructions were received from Bde that advance would be continued on the following day to COMINES CANAL, HOUTHEM being this batt' objective. The advance was to commence at 7.10 a.m. the disposition of Batt were then as follows. D Coy in front line, B Coy in support, followed by A Coy. C Coy in reserve. | |
| | | | up to 12 midnight 9 M.Gs, 17 PRISONERS (2nd Lt V S BURTT from Coys.) | App 4/7 |
| | | MESSINES were captured with small opposition & the Batt made good progress towards HOUTHEM, object being to secure the canal crossing. 1 M.G. and 1 FIELD GUN captured at MESSINES. | 82 |
| | | | Few casualties were sustained from enemy shells on E slopes of MESSINES RIDGE. Information was received at midday that 41st Div had crossed the COMINES CANAL and were moving Southwards & then struck S.E. to form flank guard to Div. A line facing S.E. South of HOUTHEM was held during the night. The 9th Lan | |

# WAR DIARY
## or
## INTELLIGENCE SUMMARY
(Erase heading not required.)

Army Form C. 2118.

| Place | Date | Hour | Summary of Events and Information | Remarks and references to Appendices |
|---|---|---|---|---|
| | | | Regt came up on right flank to fill gap between Batt. & 31st Div who has now relieved up at WARNETON. Casualties during operation 12 O/Rs killed 40 O/Rs wounded. CAPT E.H. DU HEAUME & 3 O/Rs wounded remained at duty. 2nd Lt H.J. MALLETT from tune. | P.K. |
| 03.b.3.b. | 30/9/18 | | Line reorganised & Batt remained in support to 2/14 Ln Regt. Wend received that BULGARIA had declared peace. CAPT H.T.G. BACK Total Captures 11-77mm guns 19/9/18 to U.15. 19/9/18. 3-10 cms, 10 machine guns, 1 light trench mortar | Poss. |

M W Page. Lt Col.
Comdg 9/10 London Regt.

Appendix I

O/c Coy -

The Battn will relieve the
7/23rd LR at DONEGAL FARM –
N.31.d - as per instructions issued
at this morning's conference.

The Battn will pass starting
point - M.17.c.4.2 at 2.15 pm
100 yds interval between Coys –
50 yds between platoons. Route
via LOCRE.

Battn HQ will be at head
of column.

SCHALL
Capt & Adj
7/9

App II

Batt. Orders.                    Sunday 8/9/18.

1. Reveille 7 am  Breakfast 7.30 am
   Sick Parade 8.30 am
2. The 90th Bde will move back to Divl
Reserve in the MONT ROUGE – MONT NOIR
area tomorrow.
   The Battn will move into the area previously
occupied by the 1/6th Ches. Regt at MONT
VIDAIGNE – HQ. M.21.a.5.4.  Order of march
HQ. A. B. C. D.  HQ will move off at 3.30 pm
& the other Coys at 10 min intervals. Distance
of 200 yds to be maintained between platoons.
Advance parties of 1 officer & 5 ORks per Coy
will proceed tomorrow morning & take over
accommodation from opposite Coys & will also
arrange to meet their respective Coys at Cross
Rds. M.21.b.55.10.
   Transport  1 limber will report to each Coy
& 3 to Battn HQ at 3 pm. Teams for Cookers
will report at 1 pm. Cooks will proceed
with Field Kitchens to new area & arrange for hot
meal to be ready for troops on arrival.
   Receipts for all tents, shelters or stores taken
over to be sent to 4R by 12 noon 10th inst.
   Completion of move to be notified to 4R.

                                    S. C. HALL
                                    Captn Adjt.

App. III

S E C R E T.  COPY NO. 11

## 2/15th Battn. London Regt.

### ORDER NO. LXIII.

Map Ref. Sheet 28 S.W. 1/20,000.  19th September, 1918.

1. The 36th Division is taking over the whole Corps Front on 19/20th Sept.

2. The 90th Inf. Bde. will relieve the 109th Inf. Bde. (36th Divn.) in the HILL 63 SECTOR (U.19.b.3.4. to the River DOUVE at U.7.b.6.6.).

3. The Battn. will move to NEUVE EGLISE Area in relief of 1st & 2nd Battns. R.I.R. to-night, and will be disposed so as to be able to occupy the NEUVE EGLISE Line between T.16.c.7.3. & T.3.d.7.9. in the shortest possible space of time.
    Coys. will take over areas from Coys. as arranged by the Commanding Officer with reconnaissance party.
    Battn. H.Q. will be temporarily situated at T.16.b.9.7.
    A Sketch showing dispositions will be forwarded to Battn. H.Q. by all Coys. by 12 noon, 20th inst.

4. All Trench Stores, Trench Maps, Defence Schemes, Air Photos, details of work in progress and proposed, etc., will be taken over.

5. Completion of relief to be notified to Battn. H.Q. by B. A. B. Code.

6. O/C., Signals will take over all existing signal communications

7. Administrative instructions will be issued separately.

Capt. & Adjutant.

Issued at 3 p.m.
Copies to No. 1. C.O.
            2. O.C., "A"
            3. O.C., "B"
            4. O.C., "C"
            5. O.C., "D"
            6. O.C., "HQ"
            7. M.O.
            8. T.O.
            9. Q.M.
           10. R.S.M.
           11. War Diary.
           12. Retained.

ADMINISTRATIVE INSTRUCTIONS
To
ORDER NO. LXIII.

19th Sept., 1918.

1. The Battalion will move off in the following order, "H.Q." "D" "A" "B" "C".
H.Q. Coy. will pass the Starting Point - M.26.b.2.2. - at 7.30 pm
50 yds. interval between platoons will be maintained.
Route, via BAILLEUL.
Dress: Full Marching Order including packs.

2. Transport.
1 Lewis Gun Limber will report to each Coy. & 3 limbers will report to H.Q. Coy. at 6 p.m.
The Coy. L.G. Limbers will carry 8 Lewis Guns in bags, 10 boxes S.A.A., 20 tin boxes and 8 spare parts bags. All tin boxes now with Coys., surplus to this 20 will be dumped at Guard Tent, Bn. H.Q. by 5 pm.
Medical Cart and Officers' Mess Cart will report at Battn. H.Q. at 6 p.m. Teams for Cookers will report to Coys. at 6.30 p.m. "B" Coy. will arrange to carry H.Q. dixies. Water Carts will report filled to Battn. H.Q. at 6.30 p.m., and all empty petrol cans will be loaded on to racks. Riders will report at 7 p.m.

3. All Officers' valises will be dumped at Guard Tent, Battn. H.Q., by 5.45 p.m. One Officers' Mess Box per Coy. will be dumped at Guard Tent, at 6 p.m. All surplus mess stores will be dumped at Guard Tent at 5 p.m. All petrol tins will be dumped at Guard Tent at 5 p.m.

4. Coys. must ensure that all water bottles are full before marching off.

5. Rations for consumption on 20/21st will be issued this afternoon, and carried on the man.

6. Cooks will arrange for hot tea to be issued to the men on arrival in new area.

7. Rear Party.
Capt. F. H. DU HEAUME, & 23 Other Ranks "A" Coy. will rejoin Battalion to-morrow.
The Concert Party, the Band, and sick men as detailed by the M.O. will report to Q.M. Stores.
A Guard, consisting of Cpl. Williams & 6 men of the band, will remain behind at Battn. H.Q. until Battn. Dump is cleared.
1 N.C.O. per Coy. will be left behind to hand over tents and shelters to 2/17th Lond. Regt. Receipts to be obtained in duplicate & 1 copy forwarded to O.R. by 12 noon, 20th inst.

Capt. & Adjutant.

Issued to all recipients of Order No. LXIII.

SECRET.  Order No LXIV. App IV  23.9.18.

Map ref<sup>ce</sup> PLOEGSTEERT. 1/10000

1. On the night of the 23/24 the Bde boundaries will be readjusted. The Batt<sup>n</sup> will take over from a Batt<sup>n</sup>. of the 89<sup>th</sup> Inf Bde. that portion of the front between the river DOUVE (Inc) to the MESSINES-WULVERGHEM road (Inc)

2. Dispositions :-
   'A' Co  RIGHT.
   'C' Co  LEFT.
   'B' Co  SUPPORT.
   'D' Co  RESERVE.
   B.H.Q will be at T.6.c.7.1.
   Boundary between forward Coys will be at POINT where RAILWAY crosses trench HANBURY SUPPORT N<sup>TH</sup>
   'D' Co will remain in present position

3. One Limber will report to each of A, B, C & Hdq<sup>rs</sup> Coys at 7 P.M. for conveyance of L Guns & Amm<sup>n</sup>.

4. A, B, C & Hdq<sup>rs</sup> Coys will arrange for packs & petrol tins to be dumped at suitable area where limbers can pick them up. Place to be notified to B.O.R. by 12.15 P.M.

Overcoats will be worn.

5. <u>Rations</u>  Rations will be brought to sunken road at T.6.c.4.6 tonight at 8.P.M. C2MCs will arrange for each Platoon's rations to be placed seperately in Sand bags. Petrol tins containing tea will be taken into the line & returned in tomorrows returning ration train

6. Cos will move off in the following order:
B.H.Q — 7.45 P.M.
  C      8
  A     8.15
  B.    8.30

7. All trench stores, trench maps, Defence schemes, air photos, details of work in progress & work proposed &c will be taken over. 1 Offr per Co. will proceed in advance to take over the above & arrange for Guides. Receipts to be forwarded to B.O.R in duplicate by 12 noon 24th. A sketch showing ~~dispositions~~ disposition will be forwarded to B.H.Q by all Cos by 6.AM 24th inst

8. Completion of relief will be reported to BOR by code "HALL"

9. Liason must be established with Units from flanks. This is IMPORTANT.

10. The FORWARD Coys will arrange to patrol their respective fronts as under
   "A" Co   12.30 – 1.30 A.M.
   "C" Co   1.30 – 2.30 A.M.

11. <u>Rear party</u> – 1 N.C.O. per Co will remain behind to hand over stores taken over from the R.I.F. Receipts in duplicate to be forwarded to B.O.R. by 12 noon 24th inst.

12. O/c "D" Co will report to B.H.Q at 8 P.M. tonight & will bring copy of general instructions Ref: DUTIES of SUPPORT Battn.

S. C HALL
Captn / Adjt

Issued at 12 noon.
Copies to Coys & Q.M.

Ref: Para 4. Men proceeding on leave to-night will remain with dumps until cleared.

Secret — App V    Copy No
         Order No. LXV.
Map. Ref: Ploegsteert 1/10000.

1. On the night 26/27th the Brigade boundaries will be readjusted. The Battn will take over from a Battn of the 89th Bde the front from the STINKING FARM – GABION FARM RD (excl) to the WULVERGHEM-MESSINES RD (incl).

2. Coys will move off in the following order:-
   HQ 10.30 pm. C 10.45 pm. A 11 pm. B 11.15 pm.
   D Coy will remain in their present position.

3. Dispositions.   C Coy on the Right
                   A Coy    "    left.
                   B Coy   Support
                   D Coy   Reserve.
                   BHQ at  T.6.C.7.1.
   Boundary between Forward Coys will be at point where Railway crosses trench HANBURY SUPPORT NTH.

4. One limber will report to each of A. B. C. & HK Coys at 9.30 pm for conveyance of Lewis Guns, S.A.A. etc. Offs. Mess Cart will be at EMU CAMP Corner at 9.30 pm & will pick up mess boxes of 'A' & B Coys. Mess Cart will report to BHQ at 9.45 pm.

5. Packs will be carried. All petrol tins are to be dumped at suitable place where limbers can pick them up. Place & no. of tins to be notified to O/R men proceeding

on leave will be left in charge of these dumps until same have been cleared by returning ration train.

6. Rations. QM will arrange for rations to be brought to Bunker Rd at T.6.c.4.6 tomorrow night at 10 pm. CQMS's will arrange for each platoon's rations to be placed separately in sand bags. Petrol tins containing tea will be taken into the line & returned on the following night.

7. Advance Party. 1 Offr per Coy will proceed in advance & take over all trench stores, trench maps, defence schemes, air photos, details of work in progress & work proposed &c. Receipts to be forwarded to BOR in duplicate by 9 am 27th.

Sketch showing dispositions will also be forwarded at same time.

Guides will be arranged for dusk by O.C Coys.

8. Completion of relief will reported to BOR by code (~~~~~~)(ENOS)

9. Liaison must be established with Units on flanks. This is important.

10. Forward Coys will arrange to patrol their respective fronts as under.
A Coy 2.30 - 3.30 am. C Coy 1.30 - 2.30 am. Patrol reports to be furnished to BoR by 6 am on proformas issued.

11. Rear Party. 1 NCO per Coy will remain

Amendments to Order No LXX     26/9/18

Ref: para 2 & 6  Coys must be prepared to move at 7.45 pm. Ration limbers will report to Coys at 7.45 pm. Hot tea will be issued to Coys at 7.45 pm & after this meal Coys will move off to the line independently at the following times:-
  C Coy 8.15 pm   A Coy 8.30 pm
  B Coy 8.45 pm

Rations will be carried on front half of limbers. The rear half will carry Lewis guns & magazines. Limbers will proceed with Coys as far as Sunken Rd about T.6.c.4.6. from which point contents will be man handled. Limbers will then return to Coy dumps in present areas & bring up S.A.A. remainder of stores & mess tins. CQMS's will proceed with limbers on second journey & arrange for limbers to be unloaded at T.6.c.4.6. CQMS's will remain with these dumps until cleared by Coy's carrying parties. Limbers will return to Coys present areas & collect all empty petrol tins &c for return to QM Stores. 2 bandsmen per Coy & men proceeding on leave will assist CQMS's in unloading & loading.

behind to hand over stores taken
over from the RIF & will rejoin Coy as
soon as possible. Receipts in duplicate
to be forwarded to BOR by 9 am 27th

S.C HALL
Capt & Adjt

Copies to all Coys & QM

Ref: pa 7   Guides

1 Guide per platoon + 1 per Coy
HQ. will be on road at T.6.c.4.6
to meet Coys

S C HALL
Capt A/Adj

(4)

7. Artillery Barrage details to follow.
8. M.G.s. Lt group (B coy 35th Bn M.G.C.) will cover Bde advance from Hill 63 in T.12.d & T.18.b.
   There will be one mobile MG coy in reserve ready to push on in support of the Infantry Adv gds.
9. T.M.Bs. Two mobile guns will advance with the leading Bns along inter Battn boundary & will be ready to support either Battn.
10. For R.A.F.; Communications, Prisoners, Intelligence Sychronisation of watches, Liason & Reports see orders for phase 1.
11. Signals.  Held up  Blue smoke Rifle grenade
    Final objective Red smoke  do.
12. The final objectives will be consolidated under cover of small detached posts. Liason with left & right Bn will be obtained.
    Picks & shovels will be carried by Support & Reserve Coys who will be responsible for getting them up to front line. Support coy will assist consolidation if heavy casualties occur in leading coys.
13. Counter attacks  D. coy will be responsible for counter attacks & flank attacks.
14. B.HQ will move from present location to Adv HQ (place to be notified later) when the village of MESSINES is captured.

OCS11 Bentie
Major

Admin. Instrns. to Order LXVI

27.9.18

1. AMMUNITION.
   (a) 1 extra bandolier will be carried by each rifleman. The 10 boxes SAA already in possession of Coys will be utilised for this purpose.
   (b) 16 Lewis Gun magazines per Lewis Gun will be carried forward.
   Any surplus SAA or L.G. mags will be dumped at Coy HQ. This will constitute Coy Reserve.
   (c) Bombs. Each rifle-man will carry 2 Mills Grenades No. 23.
   (d) Rifle Grenades. 5 Mills grenades No 23 will be issued to 2 men in each rifle section.
   (e) Smoke Bombs will be issued to rifle grenadiers on the same scale as (d).

2. WIRE CUTTERS. All available wire cutters will be carried. D Coy will hand over 11 wire cutters to A Coy.

3. AEROPLANE FLARES. 1 tin containing 2 flares will be carried by every other man.

4. AEROPLANE DISCS. All ranks must be in possession of aeroplane Discs.

5. VERY LIGHT PISTOLS. All officers & each Lewis Gun Section will carry Very Pistols, and 6 Very Lights.

6. SPECIAL SIGNALS. Special signals will be carried by A & C Coys. 3 will be issued to each platoon & 3 to Coy H.Q. 24 will be kept at Battn HQ
   Special signals will be :- Signals (white/white/white)
                                Red smoke bombs
                                Blue smoke bombs.

7. MESSAGE ROCKETS. 4 Message Rockets will be issued to A & C Coys.

8. PICKS & SHOVELS. Support & Reserve Coys will each carry 24 picks & 48 shovels.

9. RATIONS. 2 days rations will be issued tonight. Each man will carry unexpended portion of day's ration plus 2 days rations plus Iron Ration.

10. WATER. Water will be brought up in Petrol Tins tonight & each man must have a full water bottle at ZERO hour on 'J' day.

11. DUMPS. All packs will be dumped at Coy HQ by midnight, 27th inst. Men proceeding on leave tomorrow will remain in charge of these dumps. The QM will detail 4 men per Coy from Rear HQ to move these dumps on to WULVERGHEM - MESSINES RD.

12. CARRYING PARTIES. 'D' Coy will provide 2 parties of 1 Sgt & 25 o/Rks each to be at T.6.c.4.6 at 9 pm tonight, 27th inst, to carry stores as per attached schedule to A & C Coys. Each Coy will provide its own ration party. A & C Coys will arrange for guides to be at T.6.c.4.6 at 9 pm.

13. R.A.P. The R.A.P will be situated at T.5.d.95.40

J C Hall
Capt & Adj

Secret F    (1)    App VI

*Not to be taken beyond*
*Coy HQ*

Copy no 3

Order no LXVI by    27.9.18

Major A.C.H. Benke M.C. (commdg)

2/5 London Rgt.

1. **Information** 1(a) Information has been obtained pointing to the probability of the enemy withdrawing in the near future from his present front to positions beyond the MESSINES - WHTSCHAETE ridge or still further East. It is possible that a bold & aggressive action on our part may bring about this withdrawal.

    (b) The day on which this withdrawal may commence will be known as "J" day.

2. **Intention** 2. The Battalion will be prepared to advance on "J" day in conjunction with troops on either flanks and press the enemy if signs of hostile withdrawal are observed. It is the intention of the Commanding Officer to press close on the heels of the retreating enemy but avoiding casualties as far as possible.

3. **Phases** The advance will be carried out in two phases.

    (1) "A" & "C" coys will secure the line from U.1.b.35.45 to U.1.d.90.60.

    (2) The Battalion will advance at A L hours on the order being given from Bn HQ. and cooperate with units of both flanks and secure the line O.33.b.70.40 to U.H.a.45.45 and consolidate this objective.

(2)

4. <u>Boundaries</u>. The N boundary for the Bn is as follows:- T 6 d 75.45 and thence along the WULVERGHEM - MESSINES road (inclusive) to O 33 c 30.45 — O 33 c 65.55 and thence along track (inclusive) O 33 d 74.45

The S. boundary for the Battalion is as follows U 1 d 6.0 - U 1 d 9.2 - U 3 a 1.1 - U 3 a 8.4 - U 4 a 5.8.

The dividing line between A and B coy is a line from U 1 c 95. 55 to O 33 d 90 - 55.

<u>FIRST PHASE</u> The Companies in the line will carry out this phase. 'A' coy on the left and 'B' on the right.

1. Before dawn A coy will clear all troops from their front line and the following dispositions will be taken up.

(a) A coy. 2 platoons will move to their right and occupy front trench from U1C 70-60 U 1 C 90.30.

(b) A coy will then have 2 platoons in support in King Edward Trench.

(c) B coy will close its 2 platoons in the front line to the right to make room for the two platoons of 'A' coy mentioned in 1.(a).

(d) B coy will have one platoon in immediate support in CALGARY AVENUE E.

(e) B coy will have one platoon in reserve in trench running N-S at western end of CALGARY avenue E.

(f) B coy will be in support in STH MIDLAND FARM area

(g) D coy will be Battalion Reserve

(3)

(2) At ZERO 'A' coy will send out two fighting patrols to to secure BIG BULL COTTAGE and occupied area H.1.d.4.7 - U.1.d.2.9.

One platoon will remain in immediate support to these patrols, in front line.

~~The support platoons of 'A' coy in King Edward Trench will send forward a fighting patrol to BOYLE'S FARM to secure the left flank. The remainder of these two platoons will the move forward to front line when BIG BULL COTTAGE has been secured.~~

'C' coy will cooperate with this operation and send out a fighting patrol to ROME ALLEY area to protect right flank of the attack

'C' coy will then have one platoon in immediate support and two platoons as in 1(d) and (e)

'B' coy will remain in Sth MIDLAND FARM area until further orders are issued

3. When these objectives have been gained OC's 'A' and 'C' will arrange small posts for defence and ensure their respective flanks are secured.

4. No advance beyond the "Steenbeck" will be made even in the event of a hostile withdrawal.

5. Should the enemy have vacated the objective given the fighting patrols will try + get in touch with enemy but not beyond the limit stated in 4.

(4)

6. Troops on the LEFT but not on the RIGHT will cooperate in phase 1.

7. REPORTS must be sent at once and at frequent intervals from the attacking parties and the front line O.Ps.

8. ARTILLERY
   (a) H-3 to H
       2 guns B/149 engage BIG BULL COTTAGE (U.1.d.0.9)
   (b) H-3 to H+2
       B/149 barrage trench U.1.b.15.15 to U.1.d.45.75
       The 2 guns firing (a) join in this barrage at H.
       C/149 barrage trench U.1.d.45.75 to U.2.c.0.40
   (c) H+2 to H+3.
       B/149 barrage from U.1.b.2.3 to U.1.d.7.9 concentrating 3 guns on U.1.d.6.9
       C/149 barrage from U.1.d.7.9 to U.2.c.2.4
   (d) H+3 to H+10.
       Barrage on general line U.2.c.5.6. — U.2.a.a.1.3 — U.1.b.7.6.

9. MACHINE GUNS. (a) H-5 to H.
       H.M.Gs. fire from T.6.b on BIG BULL COTT.
   (b) H to H+15.
       Same guns fire on U.1.b.50.45.

10. L.T.M.B. (a) Previous to H-5 all L.T.Ms in action will be at disposal of O.C. Battn
    (b) H-5 to H-1
        "A" group (2 guns) on BIG BULL COTTAGE
        "B" group (2 guns) on U.1.d.33.80
    (c) H-1 to H+10
        "A" group (2 guns) on U.1.d.65.90
    (d) H to H+11
        "B" group (2 guns) on U.1.d.65.60

11. HEAVY ARTILLERY is firing a creeping barrage commencing at H hour to assist fighting patrols.

(5)

12. <u>R.A.F.</u> The most advanced infantry will indicate their positions by tin discs & RED flares on a call from the aeroplane.

13. <u>Communications</u> will be maintained by flag, shutters, and runners.

14. <u>Signals</u> (Bn) (a) White very lights indicate "Objective gained"
    (b) Signal Rifle Grenades blue smoke "Am held up"

15. <u>Prisoners</u> and Intelligence from captured documents will be immediately sent to Battn H.Q.

16. <u>Liason</u> with flanks must be established

17. <u>Watches</u> will be synchronised at midnight 27/28

18. <u>Zero</u> will be notified to coy commanders verbally.

19. <u>Bn H.Q.</u> at present location at T 6 c 7.1.

20. <u>If</u> the attack is unsuccessful a further determined effort will be made at 7.30 pm Further instructions on this point will be issued.

A C St Bertie
Major
Commdg 2/15 London Regt

Capt Adjutant

## 2nd PHASE

1. Should the 1st Phase be successful an attack will be made on the right by the 31st Division with the 2/14th London Regt protecting their left flank. The attack will commence at Z hrs on 'S' day. Not more than 3 hrs notice can be given of Z hour.

2. On the receipt of orders and in conjunction with the attack mentioned in para 1, the Battn will be ready to advance to its final objectives by a series of bounds as follows:-
   (1) Trench line U16 35 40 – U2c 00 80 (starting pt)
   (2) Line O32c 40 05 – U2a 40 75
   (3) Line O33c 35 50 – U3a 90 40
   (4) Final objective (O33b 70 no) – (U4 a 85 75)

3. A report will be rendered at the completion of each bound by the communications available.

4. White Very lights will also be fired by advanced troops when a bound is completed.

5. Aeroplane flares RED will be lit by ADVANCED TROOPS ONLY when called for by aeroplanes.

6. Formation. General outline.

(advance general bearing of 80° Mag.)

```
     <— A coy 400° —>     <— B coy 400° —>
      b   b   b   b         b   b   b   b
Line of strong
fighting patrols    ↑
                   150x
                    ↓
      b   b   b   b
                    ↑
                   100x
                    ↓                As for 'A' coy
This line is →   b   b   b   b
responsible for
liaison.           ↑
                  150x
                    ↓
      b   b   b   b
                    ↑
                   100
                    ↓
                 Coy HQ

         — B coy (2 plns) —     — B (2 plns) —
2 platoons →  b   b   b   b       b   b   b   b
on whole front     ↑                  ↑
                  150x               150x
← do. →            ↓                  ↓
              b   b   b   b       b   b   b   b
                    ↑                 ↑
                   100               100
                    ↓                 ↓
                         Coy HQ

     Art formn          B coy         Art formn
                      Bn Reserve

                        B.HQ
```

Amendments to Order No LXVI   G

Arrangements for covering fire at "L" hour :-
(a) The artillery barrage will open on the
line U.8.c.0.0 – U.8.a.0.1 – U.8.a.2.6 –
U.2.c.2.1 – U.2.c.2.3 – U.1.d.7.5 –
and will remain on that line for 8 minutes.

The barrage will then move forward
at the rate of 100ˣ in 3 minutes, in
conjunction with the barrage on the right
as far as the line U.8.d.5.6 – U.8.b.70.55.

No white Very lights will be used by
night for signal purposes.

NOTE ALTERATION + substitute

BLUE SMOKE BY DAY = HAVE REACHED BDE
                         OBJECTIVE

RED SMOKE BY DAY = AM HELD UP BY
                         ENEMY

WHITE/WHITE/WHITE BY NIGHT   Cancelled.

By night no light signals will be allowed
except for the recognised S.O.S.

At 7.30 pm on 'J' Day if no withdrawal of the enemy has been observed, the Infantry will go forward under cover of the following barrage:-

A/149 Battery    U.1.b.3.3 to U.1.d.95.90.
D/149 Battery 2 Hows. U.1.d.95.50 to U.2.c.25.50
B/149 Battery    U.2.c.25.50 to U.2.d.0.1.
D/149 Battery 4 Hows. U.2.d.0.1 to U.8.b.7.8.
C/149 Battery    U.8.b.7.8 to U.8.b.55.00

This Barrage will lift 200 yds every 3 minutes, until the following line is reached, on which it will remain for 6 minutes:-

A/149 Battery    O.33.b.7.4 to O.33.d.95.60
D/149 Battery 2 Hows. O.33.d.95.60 to O.34.c.1.1.
B/149 Battery    O.34.c.1.1 to U.4.a.7.7
D/149 Battery 4 Hows U.4.a.7.7 to U.4.c.7.8
C/149 Battery    U.4.c.7.8 to U.10.a.6.5

     RATES OF FIRE   "RAPID"

Allotation of Barrages.
1. Artillery
  (a) H to H plus 3.
  2 guns B/149 engage BIG BULL COTTAGE (U.1.d.0.9)
  (b) H to H plus 5.
  B/149 Barrage Trench from U.1.b.15.15 to
U.1.d.45.75, the 2 guns firing as in (a) join
in their barrage at H plus 3.
  C/149 Barrage Trench from U.1.d.45.75 to
U.2.c.04.40
  (c) H plus 5 to H plus 6
  B/149 barrage from U.1.b.2.3 to U.1.d.7.9
(concentrating 3 guns on U.1.d.6.9).
  C/149 barrage from U.1.d.7.9 to U.2.c.2.4
  (d) H plus 6 to H plus 12
  B/149 barrage from U.1.b.5.5 to U.2.a.0.1.
  C/149 barrage from U.2.a.0.1 to U.2.c.4.6.

B Battery will fire one Incendiary Shell
at H Hour on U.1.d.45.75

Rates of fire INTENSE 75% H.E.

2. M.Gs.
 (a) H to H plus 3.
    4 M.G's fire from T.6.b. on BIG BULL COTTAGE.
 (b) H plus 3 to H plus 18.
    Same guns fire on U.1.b.50.45.

3. L.T.M's.
 (a) H to H plus 3.
    All 4 guns on BIG BULL COTTAGE, U.1.d.0.9.

 (b) H plus 3 to H plus 5.
    All 4 guns on U.1.d.60.95 to U.1.d.95.70.

"L" hour will be notified to all concerned by a code phrase, e.g. "Received your L/14/45" will mean L hour is at 14.45 or 2.45 pm.
  e.g. "Received your L/10/30" will mean
    "L" hour is at 10.30 am
 a.m. and p.m. will NOT be used.
The 24 hour system will be used.

---

You will go forward at ZERO in conjunction with these barrages. Please acknowledge

R. W. Benth[?]
Major

Issued at 3 am
 to all concerned.

Copy ~~ORDER NO LXVII~~ H

5.43 P.M. "Aparvé"

The Boshes are reported to be returning at 6·30 P.M. A + C. Companies will push out patrols to get in touch with enemy. The people on left will have Artillery Barrage but none on our sector unless ordered. If these patrols can push on a small advance guard will take ~~U3 a 0.4~~ to U3a 5.0.

high ground west of Mossimer. Great Importance is attached to liason with flanks.
Frequent reports must be sent.

ORDER NO LXVIII                    I

Copy Warning Order aaa The Bde will advance tomorrow 5.30 am & COMINES CANAL aaa DIVIS will at once reorganise ready to advance on line EAST from PETITE DOUVE FARM – U.8. central aaa DASA GABION FARM – SNIPERS HOUSE – RUINED Bo
of PIRE aaa Axis of advance ??? aaa Boundaries Southern Divisional Boundary, U.10. a P.7 – through new posts O.35.C.7.3 inclusive then straight line to COMINES CANAL at P.20.c.9.2 aaa Northern Boundary, Present boundary to O.34.b.0.5 then in straight line to bridge at HOUTHEM BRIDGE inclusive to 70th Bde at P.19.d.3.4 aaa Bn boundary, 6 Bn boundary – U.a.a.1.7 – O.35.a.4.4 – O.29 central to bridge at P.20.d.4.0 aaa bridge r road inclusive to Left Bn

Acknowledge
Map herewith

Batt. Orders                  29.9.18

The Batt. will advance through
MESSINES & HOUTHEM
today at 5.30 a.m.
2nd Army 65°
Ljcoon and Fenole will be
established immediately
The order for advancing
Reports should be inward
+ will be sent in order
as follows
    D & B   A
        & C     A & C
            A & C
            C & D 4 O

The Batts. will advance
in the following order

D   firing line
B   support
A   support
      behind B.
C   Reserve

At least 200 yds between
the 3 leading companies
Reserve 500 yds behind A.
D coy will provide screen
+ advance guard
The remainder will follow in
small blobs

Alex Bank
Major

Issue to Coys at 2.45 am

SECRET.    VOLUME NO. IV.

WAR   DIARY

of the

2/15th BATTALION LONDON REGIMENT (P.W.O.) CIVIL SERVICE RIFLES

for the month of

OCTOBER, 1918.

IN THE FIELD.
1st Nov., 1918.

Lt.-Colonel
Cmdg. 2/15th Battn. London Regiment.

Army Form C. 2118.

# WAR DIARY
or
## INTELLIGENCE SUMMARY.
(Erase heading not required.)

Instructions regarding War Diaries and Intelligence Summaries are contained in F.S. Regs., Part II. and the Staff Manual respectively. Title pages will be prepared in manuscript.

| Place | Date | Hour | Summary of Events and Information | Remarks and references to Appendices |
|---|---|---|---|---|
| MAP REFERENCE BELGIUM SHEET 28 1/20000 | | | | |
| 036.b.3.7 | 1/10/18 | | Batt in support to 2/14 LON REGT. Enemy artillery active Batt H.Qrs shelled, casualties 2 O/Rs killed, 3 O/Rs wounded. Crews received that Batt would be relieved on the 2nd inst. & that 10.Rs. would concentrate in area O.21.b. Base to be in South Reserve. | DOK |
| | 2/10/18 | | Batt relieved by 33rd LON REGT at 2 a.m. & camped in area received at about O.27.a. | APP I. SAR |
| O.27.a | 3/10/18 | | Persistent shelling of Batt area from 10 p.m. to 12.30 p.m. causing casualties. 1 O/R killed, 3 O/Rs wounded. Crews received from Bde to move Bns A Qrs B, C & D Coys moved forward O.14.c.8.2 to new area. | DSR |
| O.14.c.8.2 | 4/10/18 | | Batt engaged for work under C.R.E. repairing roads. 2nd Lt G.L. BONNIER reported from Training under Corps arrangements. | DOK |
| | 5/10/18 | | L.G. COURSE. Zeppelin carried out trial scheme under Bde arrangements. | SAR |
| | 6/10/18 | | Training. Lt H. ARUNDEL joined Reception Camp from GEN COURSE & went to hospital. | SAR |
| | 7/10/18 | | Training. Crews received to move of Divisional cavalry. | DSR |

# WAR DIARY
## or
## INTELLIGENCE SUMMARY.
(Erase heading not required.)

Army Form C. 2118.

| Place | Date | Hour | Summary of Events and Information | Remarks and references to Appendices |
|---|---|---|---|---|
| O.14.b.0.4. | 8/10/18 | | Training under reorganisation. Lt A WHITING rejoined from G.A.S. course and assumed command of C. Coy. Batt moved under canvas at O.14.b.0.4. B, C + D Coys billeted at WULVERGHEM. A.C.H. BENKE M.C. assumed command of Batt LT COL A.W. GAZE MC to Staff Course, CAMBERLEY, U.K. | |
| | 9/10/18 | | Working parties Two Coys at work on roads. Remainder training. | 80% |
| - | 10/10/18 | | Training. Warning orders received that 90" BDE intended relieving left frontline June of 89' BDE on night of 14/12" Medical inspection. MAJOR A.C.H. BENKE M.C. granted permission to attend Boards of work of Lt Col during absence of LT COL A W GAZE M.C. to Staff Course. | 80% |
| - | 14/10/18 | | Batt left camp at 10.30 hours to relief 2/8 B.I.F at AFRICA Q.13.2.3.7 when at O.22.d.3.8 orders were received to remain there until dusk. The Batt left at 19.00 hrs & relief was completed at 0330 hrs. No casualties during relief. C.S.M. DYER and C/Sgt BROWN. 2nd Lt G. L. BONNER to U.K. | 80% |

Army Form C. 2118.

# WAR DIARY
## or
## INTELLIGENCE SUMMARY.
(Erase heading not required.)

Instructions regarding War Diaries and Intelligence Summaries are contained in F. S. Regs., Part II. and the Staff Manual respectively. Title pages will be prepared in manuscript.

| Place | Date | Hour | Summary of Events and Information | Remarks and references to Appendices |
|---|---|---|---|---|
| Q.18.c.3.7 | 12/10/18 | | Enemy artillery active. Orders received that 90º Inf. Bde. would attack & capture the battle position on a frontage of the front between W.18.V.1.6 and GHELUWE (Q.13.c.2.9 to Q.9.c.0.2) on the 14th inst. This Batt. to attack on the right, 2/16 Lon.Rigt on the left, 2/16 Lon Regt in reserve. | |
| | 13/10/18 | | Aerial circus for attacks issues. DISPOSITIONS of coys. B & D coys APP I on the line, C Coy in SUPPORT and A Coy in RESERVE. | |
| | | | L.TH ARUNDEL to Reynolds | |
| | 14/10/18 | | Enemy heavily gun shelled front line and area near Batt. H.Qrs. At 05.35 Barrage opened & at 05.38 B & D coys moved to attack. Enemy artillery replied very heavily and promptly. At 07.00 Runner Right T. coy (D coy) reported by pigeon objective gained, firing on to railway in Q.21 and Q.22. B Coy on the left reported objective gained & in touch with both flanks. At 07.40 Runner A Coy moved up to old front line. C Coy were in close support to two forward coys. D Coy had to move back from | |

# WAR DIARY or INTELLIGENCE SUMMARY.

Army Form C. 2118.

(Erase heading not required.)

| Place | Date | Hour | Summary of Events and Information | Remarks and references to Appendices |
|---|---|---|---|---|
| Q.13.a.2.7. | 14/10/18 | | railway owing to M.G. fire from right rear. B. Coy reported 1000 yds whole line held up & Batts on right & left clearing line. Batt consolidated line gained & pushed patrols forward. Total prisoners 9 Officers 306 O/Rs — Enemies 7 O/Rs killed, 35 O/Rs wounded. The enemy was fairly quiet on the front during the night. Our patrols very active & endeavoured to reach the RIVER LYS. Enemy shelling area considerably during the night — a great deal gas shelling was experienced over whole area. | 800 |
| Q.13.a.3.7. | 15/10/18 | | Patrols reached the RIVER LYS and C. Coy pushed through B & D Coys & came to hold ground gained. Batt to advance to Q.14.b.9.a. Orders received that 9/16 LON. R. & GT reverted to be over whole left front & Batt to move fresh into RESERVE at TENBRIELEN & Batt to cross the RIVER LYS at BOUSBECQUE and hold ground S. of same. Bridges at this front reported swinging. Information received that B. & E. on At 16.40 relief cancelled |

**Army Form C. 2118.**

# WAR DIARY
## or
## INTELLIGENCE SUMMARY.
*(Erase heading not required.)*

| Place | Date | Hour | Summary of Events and Information | Remarks and references to Appendices |
|---|---|---|---|---|
| Q.14.b.9.4. | 16/10/18. | | A COY successfully cleared BOUSBECQUE of enemy + took up position Q35 b.9.c Q34 to W.H.a, the left flank resting on the RIVER LYS. C COY were sent forward to fill gap between A COY and the left sub sector of the right brigade. Enemy holding the LINSELLES SWITCH LINE and RONCQ LINE. M.G.'s active. D COY moved across the river in support during the night. The right brigade took over C COY's front and C COY withdrew to north side of river. B COY relieved A COY. Bridge Sgt. LAW BURCH to hospital. | A COY were ordered to cross the river near WERVICQ and form bridgeheads N of BOUSBECQUE while the R.E.'s bridged the river. Bridge successfully constructed & C COY moved across the support to A COY. 2nd Lt W.P. WEBB transferred to 15.2.1918. |
| " | 17/10/18 | | Information received that enemy were retiring on our flanks. B COY pushed patrols forward and at 1300 hrs the Batt moved forward in | |

(6175) W1 W253/P56 60,000 12/7 D.D. & L. Sch 575. Forms/C2118/15

# WAR DIARY
## or
## INTELLIGENCE SUMMARY.
*(Erase heading not required.)*

Army Form C. 2118.

Instructions regarding War Diaries and Intelligence Summaries are contained in F. S. Regs., Part II. and the Staff Manual respectively. Title pages will be prepared in manuscript.

| Place | Date | Hour | Summary of Events and Information | Remarks and references to Appendices |
|---|---|---|---|---|
| | | | pursuit of enemy. B Coy formed the advance guard with D Coy in support. Batt to be A & C Coys moved to PAPER MILLS, BOUSBECQUE. B Coy secured the high ground E of the LINSELLE'S SWITCH LINE and A & D Coys were ordered to push on & make good the road running from HALLUIN to RONCQ. Mont ad D Coy reached RONCQ at 15.45 hours. DISPOSITIONS for the night 17/18 were as follows:— A & D COYS holding outpost line between HALLUIN and RONCQ. C COY in SUPPORT at X.12.6.10. B COY in reserve at W.6.b.2.7. once BATT HQrs at Q.36.a.3.8. | Sd |
| Q.36.a.2.8/4/4/8 | | | Orders received that 2/14 LON REGT would form through our lines at 0700 hrs. Batt to move forward in SUPPORT. Batt assembled at CROSS ROADS, MONT'D HALLUIN at 08.30 hours and marched in column of route viâ DRONKARD. Batt billetted for night in area about M.2.6 and M.3.2. Enemy planes busy all down by L.GUN fire. LT A WHITTING M.C. to be Coty Sgt. whilst commanding a Coy. 7-9-18 | |

**Army Form C. 2118.**

# WAR DIARY
## or
## INTELLIGENCE SUMMARY.
*(Erase heading not required.)*

Instructions regarding War Diaries and Intelligence Summaries are contained in F. S. Regs., Part II. and the Staff Manual respectively. Title pages will be prepared in manuscript.

| Place | Date | Hour | Summary of Events and Information | Remarks and references to Appendices |
|---|---|---|---|---|
| M32.b.6.7 | 19/10/18 | | Advance continued. Objective - The line PETIT VOISINAGE - TOURBROEK | |
| | | | KALVERSTEERT. Batt. to be ready to move at 1400 hrs. | |
| | | | Batt. moved at 1400 hrs & billeted for the night TOLPENHOEK | 810 |
| | | | area. A Coy at S.30.a.3.7. | |
| S.5.a.3.7 | 20/10/18 | | The Bde continued the advance at 07.10 hrs. Finish objective the | |
| | | | ESPIERRES - HELCHIN ROAD. Batt. in SUPPORT with | 874 |
| | | | Bn Hd. Qrs. in | |
| | | | to be ready to move to La Courbette red building about N of PETIT TOURCOING | |
| | | | at 16.00 hrs. Bn. red building about N of PETIT TOURCOING | |
| T.3.c6.L.4. | 21/10/18 | | Orders received that 70" BDE would the remainder | 874 |
| | | | of front lines. | |
| T.3.c6.L.4. | 22/10/18 | | Orders received to move to ST. GENOIS area at 1300 hrs Coys | 895 |
| | | | in billets at 16.30 hrs | |
| " " | 23/10/18 | | Batt. in Billets ready to move at 2 hours notice. | |
| " " | 24/10/18 | | Training. 2ⁿᵈ Lt S.L. MILLER & V.S. BURLL. TO U.K. on leave. 2ⁿᵈ Lt A.P. PITTAM. M.C. | 930 |
| | | | H.R. WRIGHT & 9.6 O.Rs from Base. Repated Base. CAPT B. PEALEIELD | |
| | | | awarded bar to M.C. 2ⁿᵈ Lt A.P. PITTAM & R.V. MOORE awarded M.C. | |

# WAR DIARY
## or
## INTELLIGENCE SUMMARY.
*(Erase heading not required.)*

Army Form C. 2118.

| Place | Date | Hour | Summary of Events and Information | Remarks and references to Appendices |
|---|---|---|---|---|
| T.O.C.1.H. | 25/10/18 | | Training. L/SGT R. MASON & PTE S. VOLKE awarded D.C.M. | 87th |
| | 26/10/18 | | Training. CAPT F.W. LEWIS M.C. from REST CAMP | 9 |
| | 27/10/18 | | Batt. bathed at ROLLEGHEM. Voluntary church service at 11.00 hrs | 8 |
| | 28/10/18 | | Training. B.COY carried out advanced guard scheme at ESSEY. | 8 |
| | 29/10/18 | | D.COY do | 87th |
| | 30/10/18 | | Inspection of boys by C.O. 2nd LT H.E. CLARK to U.K. on special leave. | 8 |
| | | | 2nd LT E.N. WHEELER to hosp. | |
| | 31/10/18 | | Practice in rafting by B & D COYS. Remainder of Batt. training. 2nd LT H.B. | 87 |
| | | | WRIGHT to Vet. Course, CALAIS. CAPT A. WHITING M.C. to hospital. | |
| | | | 2nd LT G.L. BONNER from leave. R.S.M. F.E. PHILLIPS, D.S. joined for duty | |
| | | | Orders received that the Batt. would relieve 21st BDE on the line on night | |
| | 1/2 Nov | | ARMISTICE signed with TURKEY | |

Copy ?  
Lt Col  
C.O. 2/15th Battalion London Regiment,  
(P.W.O.) Civil Service Rifles.

APP. I

Secret     Order No ~~LXIII~~ 69.    1/10.18

Map Ref. 1/20000 Belgium.

1. The Battn will be relieved in the early hours of the morning by the 33rd London Regt.

2. 1½ limbers will be available for each Coy. all Coy Stores, casualty packs & petrol this must be cleared.

3. 1 Guide from each Coy HQ & 1 per platoon to report to Battn HQ at 11.30 pm
    O/C B Coy will arrange for 2 Lt Cooke to report at that time. He will be in charge of guides.

4. On completion of relief Coys will move independently to OOSTTAVERNA - O.21.b. where guides will meet the Battn. The exact location where these guides will meet Coys is uncertain.

5. Completion of relief MUST BE reported to Battn HQ

                         S.C. Hall
                         Capt & Adj

Packs will be worn.

Secret       Order No 70        APP II
          by Lt Col A C H Banks MC       Copy No

Map Ref. Sheet 28 Wervicq                    12/10/18
         28 SE 1/20000 (Sh 8a)

1. ATTACK   The Battn will attack & capture hostile
   position on the portion of the front between
   WERVICQ & GHELUWE (from Q.13.d.2.9. to
   Q.14.a.2.5)

2. FLANKS   The 1/4th London Regt will attack
   on the left & the 2/23rd on the right.

3. BOUNDARIES   N. Boundary Q.8.c.0.1 - Cross
   Rds Q.15.d.45.00 (BAD House) (excl) thence
   straight line to R LYS at Q.30 central
           S. Boundary Farm Q.13.a.15.15 (exc)
   - Farm Q.13.d.6.8 (inc) - Rd junction
   Q.14.c.80.75 (inc) - junction of road &
   track W. REEKE at Q.20.b.45.80 (excl)
   Cottages at Q.21.a.2.1 (exc) Rly junction
   Q.21.d.75.35   QUIRE Farm Q.26.a (inc)
   R LYS at Q.28.c.7.3.

4. OBJECTIVE   line of the road from
                Q.21.a.2.3 to Q.22.a.2.8

The Battn will use success signals (R.G. W/W/W) on reaching the objective. These signals will be fired from Cottages (Q.21.a.2.1) & Cross Rds Q.15.6.8.6

The Battn will exploit its success by pushing forward fighting patrols to the R. LYS immediately the protective barrage ceases. These patrols will establish themselves where they can observe all the River crossings but will not cross the Lys without further orders.

Attention of these patrols must be drawn to the fact that the bridges over the R. LYS will be kept under fire until H + 2 hrs.

5. FORMATION  D Coy — Right attacking Coy
B Coy — Left attacking Coy
C Coy — Support
D Coy — Reserve
Battn — Q.13.a.3.7

6. LIAISON  D Coy will detail 3 men at the following points to establish liaison.
REEK Village (Q.20.b.115.80)
Cottages (Q.21.a.2.1)

7. FORMING UP LINE. A line from Q.13.a.5.1 to Q.14.a.25.55 will be laid out under supervision of R.E.'s. The dividing line between Coys will be at

Q.13.b.5.5

Coys will form up on this line before 4 am on J day. The Support Coy will conform with this line at about 80-100 yds in rear.

Coys will use all available cover & dig small slits where necessary. Reserve Coy will remain in slits near B.H.Q.

8. BARRAGE (a) The attack will be covered by a creeping barrage of 18 pdr smoke, shrapnel & H.E. with 106 fuze, moving forward at the rate of 100 x' in two minutes.

Shrapnel will be used for the first lifts & H.E. after.

(b) The barrage will open at 3 minutes before H hour.

(c) 4.5" Hows & Heavy Hows will be used to deal with known occupied localities in advance of the 18 pdr barrage & to screen

WERVICQ with smoke.

(d) All bridges over the R Lys will be kept under fire from H hour to H plus 2 hours.

(e) WERVICQ Sud & Pave Bvr Hill will be gas shelled on S-1/S night with BB gas.

(f) The 18 pdr barrage map is attached.

9. M.G. SUPPORT. MGs will support the attack by barrage fire in advance of the 18 pdr barrage on known occupied localities. MG barrage fire on 90th Inf Bde front will cease at H plus 28 minutes.

10. SPECIAL Coy RE. No 4 Special RE (4" Stokes) will gas selected targets on the front of the attack on S-1/S night if wind is favourable.

No gas will be fired after midnight on S-1/S night into the area of our objective. Smoke bombs will be fired at H hour to form a smoke screen on Right Flank of 21st Inf Bde.

11. CONSOLIDATION (a) As soon as the objective is gained, the new area will be organised in depth.

(b) RE are preparing a main line of resistance on the general line BROKSTRAAT - CABARET - Q.13.d - Q.14 central - Q.15.a commencing as soon as conditions permit after the attack.

(c) One MG Coy will be in readiness to move forward to consolidate the captured ground.

12 RAF  A contact aeroplane will call for flares & discs at H plus one hour and H plus 2 hours & such other times as may be necessary according to the situation. It is of the greatest importance that the advanced troops should show their position to the contact aeroplane.

13 MEDICAL  The existing arrangements will be in force.

14 EXTRA AMMUNITION  Each man will carry 1 extra bandolier.

15. TOOLS   C & A Coy. will carry picks & shovels.

16. Prisoners of War to be sent to BHQ

17. WIRE CUTTERS   A special issue is being made to leading Coys.

18. TIME   Watches will be synchronised at midnight on night of 3-1/3

19. COMMUNICATIONS   Coys will have to rely on means of communication other than wire
   Pigeons &c will be used

20. ACKNOWLEDGE

(Sd) SCHARL
Capt - Adj

Secret    Amendments to Order No 70.    13/10/18

1. In para 4 delete the words "but will not cross the LYS until further orders" and add the following:-
   The Batln will make every endeavour to cross the R. Lys & push through BOUSBECQUE to the Southern end. Should these patrols succeed in crossing the Lys, they must be at once supported by other troops.

2. In the event of the enemy retiring & the exploitation proving successful, care must be taken in approaching the areas shown on attached sketch owing to the fact that these areas will be shelled with BB Shell (mustard gas) on 3 + 4 nights.

3. The Boundary between I Army & the 2/23rd L.R. will be amended as follows:-
   Boundaries have arun. to COTTAGES at Q.21.a.2.1 — NEERBAVICHY Farm to Right Brigade. House at R.27.b.57.2 to Left Brigade. House Q.33.d.a.b. to Left Brigade — KEITH HOUSE W.4.a.0.0 to Left Brigade.

4. In the event of a successful advance to the R.A.S the Sqn S.R will ensure contact with the Bttn on their left.

S.C. HALL
Capt S/Ldr.

Issued at 1900hrs to all recipients of O.O No 70

4. In the event of a successful advance to the R.A.S, the Sqn S.R will ensure contact with the Bttn on their left.

S.C. HALL
Capt S/Ldr.

Issued at 1900hrs to all recipients of O.O. No 70

Sketch attached to amendment
of operation orders 40

Q 21 d 0.2

Q 22 a 45 50

W 4 c 05 80

Q 3 a d
9 1

Sketch attached to amendment of operation order 40

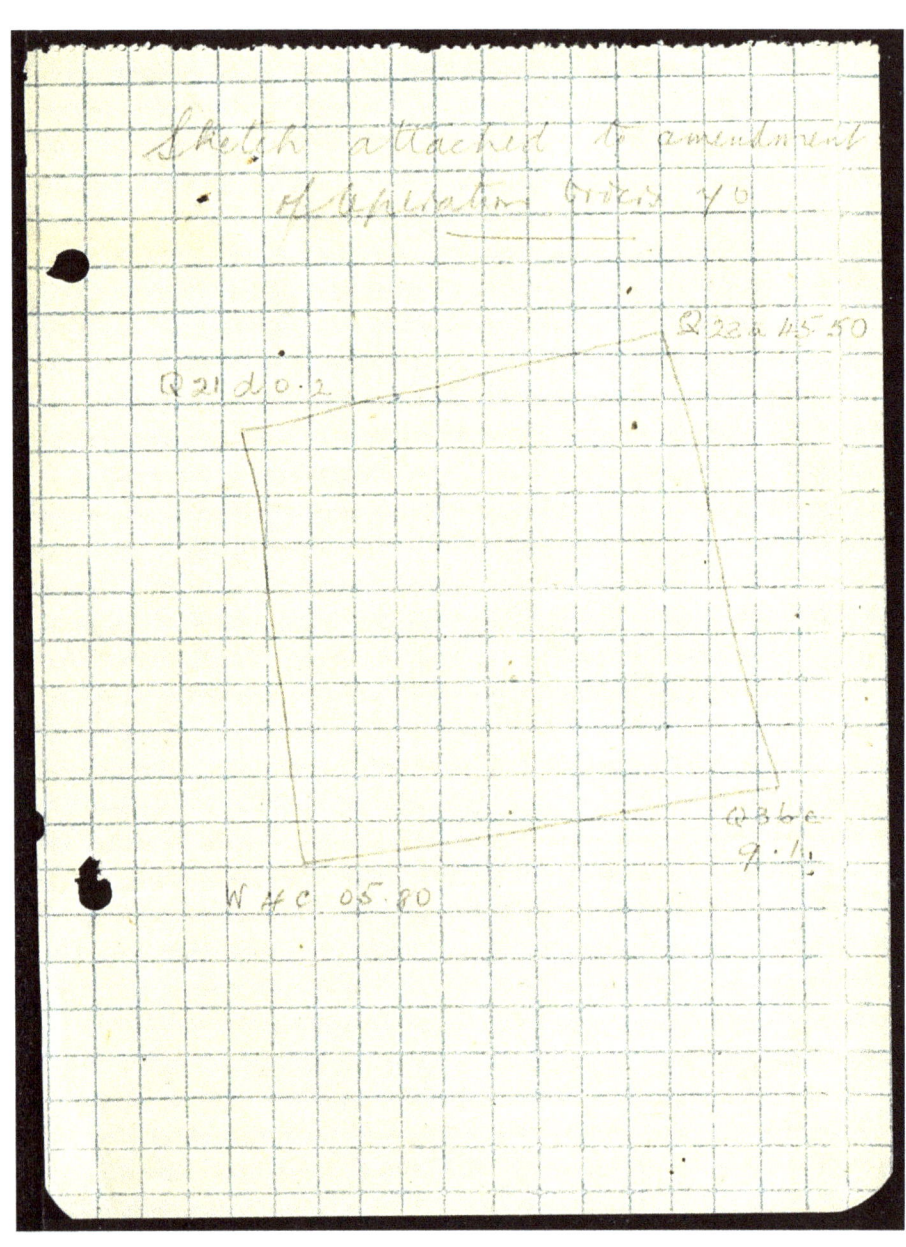

Q21 d 0.2
Q22 b 45.50
Q36 c 9.1
W 4 c 05.80

SECRET.                                    VOLUME No. 4

WAR DIARY

OF           THE

2/15th BATTALION LONDON REGT

(P.W.O., Civil Service Rifles)

for      the      month

of    NOVEMBER 1918.

                                   A.W. Gage.
                                     Lt. Col
                                       Cmg.

Army Form C. 2118.

# WAR DIARY
## or
## INTELLIGENCE SUMMARY.
(Erase heading not required.)

Instructions regarding War Diaries and Intelligence Summaries are contained in F.S. Regs., Part II. and the Staff Manual respectively. Title pages will be prepared in manuscript.

| Place | Date | Hour | Summary of Events and Information | Remarks and references to Appendices |
|---|---|---|---|---|
| T.3.d.I.H. | 1/4/18 | | Batt. moved at 1800 hrs to relief of 18th Batt. K.R.R. 122 Bde. 41st Div. on the line | S.K. |
| | | | DISPOSITIONS of COYS. B & C in front line D & A Coys in SUPPORT | |
| P.33.c.9.7. | 2/4/18 | | Relief complete at 0145 hrs. 2 O/Rs wounded. Enemy artillery very active | S.K. |
| | | 0530 hrs | at 0530 hrs. CAPT (A/Major) A.C.H. BENKE D.S.O. to be A/Lt. Col. | |
| | | | 25-10-18 whilst commanding in Italy. | |
| | 3/4/18 | | Enemy artillery & trench mortars active – special target ALVEGHEM CHURCH | S.K. |
| | | | CPL C.D. LODGE, CPL W.T.R. NASH, L/CPL E.W. BLACKABY, L/CPL C.B. HULL, PTE REUSS | |
| | | | awarded M.M. Warning order received for relief by R.INNIS F. 3 O/R. w/A | |
| | | | situation normal. SGT C.F. JONES, PTE L. BENSTEAD & PTE F. SCOTT awarded M.M. | S.K. |
| | 4/4/18 | | Relieved by 7/8 R.I.F. – proceeded to O.32.c.8.4. | S.K. |
| O.32.c.8.4. | 27/4/18 | | Warning order received to move to N.30.a.6.7. Crews counter... | |
| 6/4/18 | | | Orders received for A & D Coys to proceed to O.10.b.8.1 and V.7.b.4 respectively in support to 2/26 LON REGT who were relieving 7/8 R.I.F. Remainder of | |
| | | | Batt. to move to N.30.w. BDE RESERVE. Further orders received | S.K. |
| | | | that only one coy would proceed in support to 2/26 LON REGT. A COY | |
| | | | reported & left. | |

Army Form C. 2118.

# WAR DIARY
## or
## INTELLIGENCE SUMMARY.
(Erase heading not required.)

Instructions regarding War Diaries and Intelligence Summaries are contained in F. S. Regs., Part II. and the Staff Manual respectively. Title pages will be prepared in manuscript.

| Place | Date | Hour | Summary of Events and Information | Remarks and references to Appendices |
|---|---|---|---|---|
| N20c7 | 7/4/18 | | Batt cleaning up generally. Orders received that D coy would rejoin Batt on night 7/8. German delegate crossed our lines at GUISE | P/A |
| | 8/4/18 | | Training. D coy rejoined Batt. | P/A |
| | 9/4/18 | | Warning order received that the enemy is shortly to move at short notice. Batt to be ready to | P/A |
| | 10/4/18 | | Batt moved at 1000 hrs to HEESTEERT. Night manoeuvres of Cavalrie | S.2.8 App I |
| P.25.c.8.5. | 11/4/18 | | Information received that hostilities would cease at 1100 hrs. Thanksgiving Service held at 1500 hrs. | App II |
| | 12/4/18 | | Training under Coy arrangements. B.Coy attached to 202 F. Coy. R.E. at BSCANAFFLES. 2nd Lts MILLER & BURTT rejoined from leave | P/A |
| | 13/4/18 | | Training. Hot Baths services. Batt arrangements. 2nd Lt H. R. WRIGHT rejoined from V.E.T. Course, CALAIS. | App |
| | 14/4/18 | | Training. Orders received that Batt would move to St ANNES on the 15th. | See App III |
| | 15/4/18 | | Batt moved at 0930 hours & arrived at billets at 1330 hours. B Coy rejoined Batt. | P/A |
| N20c8H | 16/4/18 | | Training. 2nd Lt T.H.E. CLARK rejoined from UK leave | P/A |

# WAR DIARY
## or
## INTELLIGENCE SUMMARY.

*(Erase heading not required.)*

Army Form C. 2118.

Instructions regarding War Diaries and Intelligence Summaries are contained in F. S. Regs., Part II. and the Staff Manual respectively. Title pages will be prepared in manuscript.

| Place | Date | Hour | Summary of Events and Information | Remarks and references to Appendices |
|---|---|---|---|---|
| NACG F.4 | 15/4/18 | | Church Parade at 09:30 and 18:30 hours. A Coy. Lord Roberts Convent. | |
| | 16/4/18 | | S' ANNES. 2nd LT A. CHILDS to leave at HARROGATE PLACE | |
| | | | Training. 2nd LTS S.C. LANDER & E.C. HEPWORTH went on July 1/21 furlough | |
| | | | REST CAMP. 2nd LT W. BUTLER to UK leave | |
| | 19/4/18 | | Training. New draft inspected by C.O. LT W. PEARSON to B | |
| | | | Y CAPT Cecil 19.4.18 | |
| | 20/4/18 | | Morning Bn. W Rank group picture at ST ANNES at 1100 hrs. 2nd LT A.W. SINGER wounded | |
| | | | 10 Officers & 50 O/R's attended. | |
| | | | N.C. SGT LR COULTHARD, PTE W. CARNES & L/CPL S.R. RAMLEY | |
| | | | succeeded R.S.M. CAPT REATFIELD to PARIS on lve | |
| | | | PTE V.P.E. SOUTHWOOD killed by E.S.M. PROISCUTED CAMP | |
| | | | PALECOGS & FRIEND CAPT R.M. LEWIS U.K. lve | |
| | | | C. HALL. | |
| | | | Pleaded guilty. | |
| | 23/4/18 | | Training BRB CEREMONIAL DRILL. 2W/LT J. MCMAHON | |
| | | | DCM lle formed for escort to R.S.M. A/LT A.W. BURCH S/N | |
| | | | reference from Reptiles. | |

# WAR DIARY
## or
## INTELLIGENCE SUMMARY.
(Erase heading not required.)

Army Form C. 2118.

| Place | Date | Hour | Summary of Events and Information | Remarks and references to Appendices |
|---|---|---|---|---|
| N20 c 8.4 | 23/4/18 | | Training. B & C coys Red Hot baths at ST ANNE. | P.S.4 |
| " | 24/4/18 | | Voluntary Church Service | P.S.4 |
| " | 25/4/18 | | Training including Educational work | P.S.4 |
| " | 26/4/18 | | Bett Parade for presentation by G.O.C. of MEDAL RIBBONS. 2nd L.C.B. Band played SCOTTISH at RUGGER — SOMERSET joined for only. Batt played SCOTTISH for only. results 2 pts each. | P.S.4 |
| " | 27/4/18 | | Training including Conversational Lecture translation by CAPT PAINTER | S.S.4 |
| " | 28/4/18 | | — do — D coy Race Bet bathed at ST ANNE | S.S.4 |
| " | 29/4/18 | | — do — | S.S.4 |
| " | 30/4/18 | | 9.0 in C. O.E. to move to STEENBECQUE via St Sayer. Batt left billets at c.900. Rev & marched to LINSELLES | App IV S.S.4 |

Antrobus. Lt. Col.
Cdg 1/15 London Regt.

pp I

TO's Idea [illegible]
MAIN WEFSTERT [illegible] dozen
[illegible] cattle [illegible] from [illegible]
[illegible] [illegible] [illegible]
CAD [illegible] cochrane [illegible]
[illegible] NT aw'd [illegible]
be ready to march off at [illegible]
Haskell to be rocked in to
and rptd to BM by 0800 [illegible]
[illegible] to be retd to BM
by 0830.

TO will arrange for [illegible]
to be [illegible] & [illegible] to [illegible]
to coys at 09:30 (D. 00.15)
Capt [illegible] [illegible] it to
ready [illegible] SHF at [illegible]

[illegible] the [illegible]
at BHQ 0900 hrs

[signature]
10/7/45

App II

The Memorial Service will be held at 15.00 hrs this afternoon. Parade to be as strong as possible. Dress: Belts, haversacks.

Battalion + R.I. not on duty will devote the morning to cleaning up.

The C.O. expects all ranks to look as smart as possible on this afternoon parade.

Location of ground will be notified later.

J. Offott
Capt + A.

11.11.18

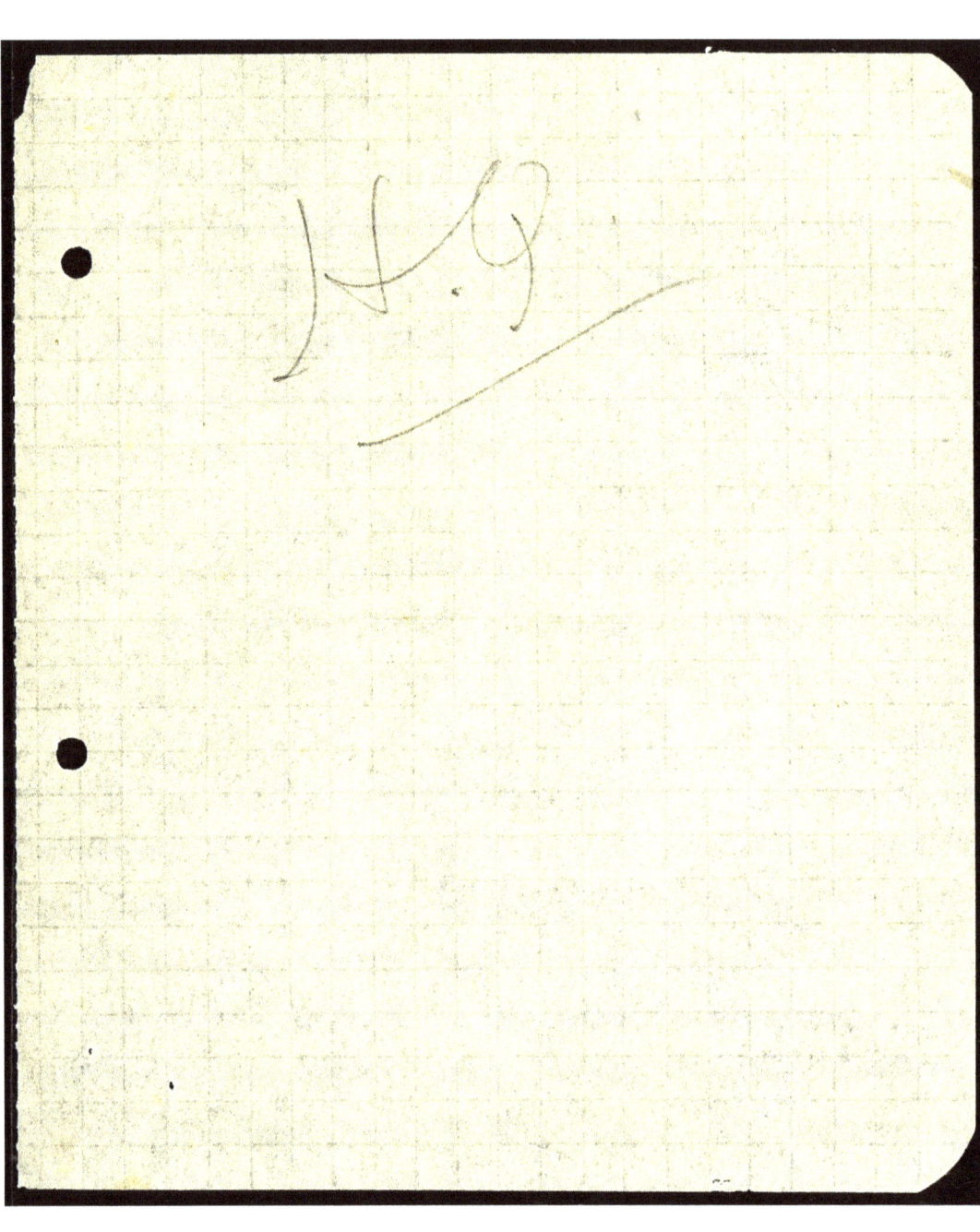

App III    War Diary

BATTALION ORDERS BY LIEUT.-COL. A.C.H. BENKE, MC., CMMDG.

Thursday, 14th November, 1918 No. 199.

1. ROUTINE. Reveille 06.00 hours.    Sick parade 08.00 hours
           Breakfast 07.30 hours.
           Lights out 21.30 hours.
   Coy. on duty "C"    Next "D".
   Officer of the day 2nd Lt. A.P. PITTAM, M.C.
   Next                 "  "  J.H. WHEATLEY, MM.

2. The battalion will move tomorrow to vicinity of ST. ANNES.
   The Battalion will form up in column of route in the following order ready to march off at 09.30 hours :-
       "H.Q.", Band, "C", "D", "A" Coys. Transport.
   Head of column - Road junction (O.30.c.1.4.)

   All blankets to be rolled in bundles of ten and dumped ready for collection at 07.00 hours.
   All Officers Valises, other than those carried on Coy. Limbers, will be returned to Q.M. Stores by 07.45 hours.

   Officers' Mounts to report at 09.00 hours.

   1 L.G. Limber per Coy. & 1 Limber and Medical Cart for H.Q. Coy. will report at 07.45 hours.

   The T.O. will arrange for Coy. Limbers and Cookers to proceed in rear of Battalion.

   DRESS. All steel helmets will be carried on backs of packs.

                                               S. C. HALL
                                           Captain & Adjutant.


   (For Part II see reverse.)

P A R T  II  O R D E R S.   Thursday, 14th November, 1918.

HOSPITAL.
537882 Pte. Hotson, W.J.   "A")
45806 Pte. Done, J.        "C")   To Field Ambulance 14-11-18.
43779 Pte. Swan, R.        "D")

STRENGTH DECREASE.
   The following sick struck off strength 14-11-18 :-
530999 Sgt. Davey, S. "D"           533789 Pte. Medland, A.S. "B"
53917 Pte. Bloomfield, H. "B"       537539 Pte. Turner, A.E. "B" X

534238 Pte. Langley, E.    "A")
45780 Pte. Tye, E.C.       "C")   To Base for Med. Board 14-11-18. S.O.S.

530616 Sgt. Henson, F.C.   "B")   To England for R.A.F. Commission 14-11-8
530612 Cpl. Endacott, A.D. "A")   struck off strength.

532610 Pte. Donau, E.B.    "D"    Adm. to hospital, England 19-10-18. S.O.S.
                                                                30-10-18.

STRENGTH INCREASE.
531136 Pte. Graham, E.W.F. "D"   From Hospital 14-11-18 taken on strength.
537539 Pte. Turner, A.E.   "B"        ditto.
545081 Pte. Hart, E.       "A"        ditto.
534503 Pte. Thomas, S.A.   "A"        ditto.
530704 Cpl. Hull, C.B.     "B"        ditto.
532836 Pte. Wallace, A.F.  "B"        ditto.

INFORMATION.
531827 Pte. Fowler, S.D.   "C"    DIED 1-11-18.
530445 Pte. Junkison, A.C. "C"    DIED 1-11-18.
533368 Pte. Williams, H.H. "D")
533793 Pte. Williams, C.J. "B")   Transferred to England 28-10-18.
530870 Sgt. Charlton, W.C. "B"    Classified 'B.2' 28-10-18.

REJOINING.
532317 L/Cpl. Cassidy, P.J. "B"   From hospital 14-11-1918.
2nd Lt. H.R. WRIGHT        "B")
533822 Pte. Jenkins, J.H.  "B")   From Course 14-11-18.
555638 L/Cpl. Gason, H.E   "D"    From Leave to U.K. 14-11-18 granted 14 days
                                    ration allowance @ 2/1 per diem.
531304 Pte. Cooper, A.     "C"        ditto.
532500 L/Cpl. Travers, R.J. "D"       ditto.
533871 Pte. Stean, W.J.    "D"    From Leave to U.K. 14-11-1918. granted 29
                                    days r.a. @ 2/1 per diem.

STRENGTH INCREASE. (Cont.)
537018 Pte. Smith, H.T.    "D"    From Leave to U.K. via Hospital 14-11-18
    Taken on strength and granted 16 days r.a. @ 2/1 per diem.

*War Diary*
*App VI*

SECRET.                                                          Copy No. 12

## 2/19th Battn. London Regt.

### Order No. LXXV.

Ref: Maps:- TOURNAI &  )
         HAZEBROUCK  a) 1/100,000
         Sheet 28    )                                     28th November, 1917.
         Sheet 28 a. ) 1/40000

1.   The 90th Inf. Brigade Group will move on the 30th November and
subsequent dates to the STEENBECQUE Area, in five stages as follows:-
         30th Nov. ...         ...    LIRBELLES area.
         1st Dec.  ...         ...    ARMENTIERES area.
         2nd Dec.  ...         ...    ESTAIRES area.
         3rd Dec.  ...         ...    ST VENANT area.
         4th Dec.  ...         ...    STEENBECQUE area.

     The general route will be:-
     a8; LIRBELLES - LEVEAU - QUERCY - LA PREVOTE - HOUPLINES -
         ARMENTIERES - SAILLY SUR LA LYS - LA CORGUE - NEUVILLE -
         ST VENANT - HAVERSKERQUE.

2.   The Battn. will form up in column of route in threes at Cross Roads
H.20.a.2.8. ready to march off at 09.10 hrs.  Order of march - H.Q., Band,
"A", "B", "C", "D", Transport.
     One hundred/will be maintained between Coys. and transport during
               yards
the first day's march.  Transport will march in rear of Battn.  Only
brakesmen and cooks will march with vehicles, all other transport
personnel will march as a formed body in rear of the transport and will come
under the orders of the officer in charge of Rear Party.

TRANSPORT ARRANGEMENTS.  One limber in addition to L.G. limber will
report to each of "A", "B", "C" & "D" Coys. to carry blankets.  Coys. will
arrange to carry valises on these L.G. limbers.  One baggage wagon will
report to H.Q. Coy. to carry cook's, signalling and orderly room stores,
H.Q. blankets and bands packs.

3.   Caps will be worn.
     Strict march discipline will be maintained at all times and the
proper halts from 00.50 to the clock hour observed.  No man may fall out
without a chit signed by an officer.

4.   The Coy. on duty will detail a rear party of 1 officer, 1 Sgt., 1 Cpl.,
1 L/Cpl. and 6 men to march in rear of transport and deal with
stragglers.

5.   Coys. will only be called to attention and 'eyes right' given to the
Divisional Commander or Brigadier once each day.

6.   The Signalling Officer will arrange to synchronise watches with
Bde. H.Q. every evening for the next day's march.

                                                          R. T. G.

7. ADVANCE PARTY. 2nd Lt. CLARK and 4 Battn. Cyclists will meet the Staff Captain at AELBEKE Cross Roads at 09.30 hrs. The T.O. will arrange for a mount for 2nd Lt. CLARK.

                                 S. C. H A L L

                                     Captain & Adjutant.

Issued at 13.00 hours.

---

| Copy No. 1 | C.O. |
| 2 | O/C. "A" Coy. |
| 3 | O/C. "B" Coy. |
| 4 | O/C. "C" Coy. |
| 5 | O/C. "D" Coy. |
| 6 | O/C. "H. Q." Coy. |
| 7 | A.M. |
| 8 | T.O. |
| 9 | M.O. |
| 10 | R.S.M. |
| 11 | Retained |
| 12 | War Diary |

SECRET.

WAR DIARY

of

2/15th BATTALION LONDON REGIMENT
(P.W.O.) Civil Service Rifles
for
DECEMBER 1918.

A. W. GAZE
Lt.-Colonel
Commanding

Army Form C. 2118.

# WAR DIARY
## or
## INTELLIGENCE SUMMARY.
(Erase heading not required.)

Instructions regarding War Diaries and Intelligence Summaries are contained in F. S. Regs., Part II. and the Staff Manual respectively. Title pages will be prepared in manuscript.

| Place | Date | Hour | Summary of Events and Information | Remarks and references to Appendices |
|---|---|---|---|---|
| HAZEBROUCK MAP | | | | |
| BOESEGHEM | 8/12/18 | | Church Service. CAPT A WHITTING from sick leave. 2nd LT J MALLETT to be Adj. Capt. 14-11-18. | 248. |
| — | 9/12/18 | | Salvage operations commenced by A. Coy. C, D & 7 Pt Salvage. B. Coy Training | 248. |
| — | 10/12/18 | | A B & HQ Coys hot bath baths at NIEPPE FOREST. C. Coy - Salvage. D. Coy - Training. Draft of 4 Officers & 124 O.R.s joined for duty. 2nd Lt A.H. STEPHENS posted to A. Coy. 2nd Lt W. P. NICOLLS to B. Coy. 2nd Lt E.J. MIALL to C. Coy and 2nd Lt B. JACKSON to D. Coy. Lt B.A. DAYTON M.C. joined for duty as Medical Officer. | 10A. |
| — | 11/12/18 | | Coys engaged on AREA IMPROVEMENTS. C. Coy Salvage. 1000 hrs S.O. instructed draft. 2nd Lt L.C. LANDER conducting Officer to party for demobilization & granted 14 days leave in UK | 11A. |
| — | 12/12/18 | | Batt. engaged on improvement scheme, erection of huts etc. | 12A. |
| — | 13/12/18 | | Area improvement Salvage. | 14A. |
| — | 14/12/18 | | do do | 14A. |

Army Form C. 2118.

# WAR DIARY
## or
## INTELLIGENCE SUMMARY.
(Erase heading not required.)

| Place | Date | Hour | Summary of Events and Information | Remarks and references to Appendices |
|---|---|---|---|---|
| Sheet 28. | | | | |
| W.23.c.1.8 | 1/12/18 | 0910 | Batt. resumed its march to BOESEGHEM and billets for the night at VERLINGHEM, arriving at 1240 hrs. HQ at J.3.b.3.8. | A.C.A. |
| Sheet 36a J.3.b.3.8. | 2/12/18 | | March continued at 0900 hrs. Batt. billets for the night at SAILLY-SUR-LA-LYS, arriving about 1500 hrs. HQ at G.17.b.1.0. | A.C.A. |
| Sheet 36a G.17.b.1.0. | 3/12/18 | | Batt. resumed its march at 0900 hrs. + billets for the night at ST VENANT | A.C.A. |
| HAZEBROUCK MAP ST VENANT | 4/12/18 | | & ST FLORIS. Batt. commenced final days march at 1245 hrs. + arrived at BOESEGHEM at 1245 hrs. HQ, A & B Coys billeted at BOESEGHEM and C & D Coys at THIENNES. LtCol A.W.GAZE, M.C. returned from CAMBERLEY COURSE. 2Lt A.E. ROBINSON to England. | AEA |
| BOESEGHEM | 5/12/18 | | Cleaning up etc. 2Lt A.W. CHILDS from HARDELOT PLAGE | ACA |
| " | 6/12/18 | | Training between Coy engagements C.O. inspected billets 2nd Lt H J MALLETT inspected CROIX DE GUERRE. d'ERPRIS (Corps) 231168 CPL B. RAMSAY " " " (BRIGADE) 531137 PTE B. GUNTON " " " (REGIMENT) | ACA |
| | 7/12/18 | | Training + improving billets | ACA |

Army Form C. 2118.

# WAR DIARY
## or
## INTELLIGENCE SUMMARY.
*(Erase heading not required.)*

Instructions regarding War Diaries and Intelligence Summaries are contained in F. S. Regs., Part II. and the Staff Manual respectively. Title pages will be prepared in manuscript.

| Place | Date | Hour | Summary of Events and Information | Remarks and references to Appendices |
|---|---|---|---|---|
| HAZEBROUCK MAP | | | | |
| BORSEGHEM | 15/12/18 | | Voluntary C of E SERVICES followed by Holy Communion. | NA. |
| " | 16/12/18 | | C. D. & TRANSPORT Race Rot baths at NIEPPE FOREST. Remainder of Bath continued with improvements. | NA. |
| " | 17/12/18 | | A, B & HQ Coy's baths. C & D Housing Salvage. 2" LT A E ROBINSON from Gertrude. | NA. |
| " | 18/12/18 | | Housing Salvage. | NA. |
| " | 19/12/18 | | Batt Route March. CORPS COMMANDER inspected A Coy's billets. 2" LT J MACMAHON. DCM. MM. granted 3 days leave to BOULOGNE | NA. |
| " | 20/12/18 | | Hutting & cleaning. | NA. |
| " | 21/12/18 | | Hutting & cleaning. | NA. |
| " | 22/12/18 | | Church Services. 2" LT J MACMAHON. DCM. MM. rejoined A & B Hutting. Numbering & Connection | NA. |
| " | 23/12/18 | | C. D. & TRANSPORT baths. C & D do do | NA. |
| " | 24/12/18 | | A, B & HQ Coy's baths. CAPT. F.W. LEWIS, M.C. to UK leave. | NA. |
| " | 25/12/18 | | Christmas Day. Church services. Officers superintended XMAS FESTIVITIES for the men. CAPT. F.H. DU HEAUME to UK leave. | NA. |

Army Form C. 2118.

# WAR DIARY
## or
## INTELLIGENCE SUMMARY.

(Erase heading not required.)

Instructions regarding War Diaries and Intelligence Summaries are contained in F.S. Regs., Part II. and the Staff Manual respectively. Title pages will be prepared in manuscript.

| Place | Date | Hour | Summary of Events and Information | Remarks and references to Appendices |
|---|---|---|---|---|
| BOESEGHEM | 26/12/18 | | NIL | |
| " | 27/12/18 | | Salvage & Education. 2ⁿᵈ Lt H.R. WRIGHT - Demobilised. 2ⁿᵈ Lts H.T. MALLETT & P. NEALL proceed on U.K. leave. | NA |
| " | 28/12/18 | | Salvage & Education. 2ⁿᵈ Lt R.V. MOORE M.C. to U.K. leave | NA |
| " | 29/12/18 | | Voluntary Church Service. 2ⁿᵈ Lt A.W. SANGER M.C. to U.K. leave. | NA |
| " | 30/12/18 | | Salvage & Education. Warning order received that Bath would probably move to ETAPLES on 1st 2nd 21st on 1st January, 1919. | NA |
| " | 31/12/18 | | do. do. | NA |

WP Cox
Lt Col
Commanding 2/15ᵗʰ London Regt

2/15th Battalion London Regiment.

# War Diary

for the month of January, 1919.

R H Andrews
Major.
Commanding 2/15th Battalion London Regiment.
(P.W.O.) Civil Service Rifles.

Army Form C. 2118.

# WAR DIARY
## or
## INTELLIGENCE SUMMARY.
(Erase heading not required.)

Instructions regarding War Diaries and Intelligence Summaries are contained in F. S. Regs., Part II. and the Staff Manual respectively. Title pages will be prepared in manuscript.

| Place | Date | Hour | Summary of Events and Information | Remarks and references to Appendices |
|---|---|---|---|---|
| BOESEGHEM | 1/1/19 | | Clearing dumps &c. Adv. party to COYECQUE. Capt. S.C. HALL to leave UK 2/Lt L.C. LANDER from leave UK | |
| BOESEGHEM | 2/1/19 | | Batt. started move to ETAPLES. Marched to COYECQUE. Arrived 15.15 hrs. | |
| COYECQUE | 3/1/19 | | Batt. resumed march to ETAPLES. Arrived HERLY-AVESNES area 14.30 hrs 1st Lt N.A. DAYTON, M.C., USR from Paris leave. Arrived ESTRELLES - D.G. Battn. | |
| HERLY-AVESNES | 4/1/19 | | — Starting point near MANINGHAM. Arrived ESTRÉE 14.45 hrs | |
| ESTRELLES-ESTREE | 5/1/19 | | Batt. resumed march to ETAPLES. Arrived LA GOUFFRE CAMP, LE TOUQUET 15.30 hrs | |
| ETAPLES LA GOUFFRE CAMP LE TOUQUET | 6/1/19 | | Cleaning up. | |
| " | 7/1/19 | | This close order drill & parental training under coy. commanders | |
| " | 8/1/19 | | do | |
| do | 9/1/19 | | Batt. at ETAPLES for rl'n to battalion. Warning order to send advance parties to CAPT. B. PEATFIELD, M.C. Batt. comm. ABANCOURT and ABBEVILLE. | |
| do | 10/1/19 | | Lt. Col. A.W. GAZE M.C. to B.d.e. 1 hr. close order drill & recreation training | |
| do | 11/1/19 | | Inspection of barracks - KiKi 2/Lts A.W. BIRCH and R.C. COOKE to England on draft conducting Move to ABANCOURT & ABBEVILLE cancelled. Warning orders for DUNKIRK | |

Army Form C. 2118.

# WAR DIARY
## or
## INTELLIGENCE SUMMARY.
(Erase heading not required.)

Instructions regarding War Diaries and Intelligence Summaries are contained in F. S. Regs., Part II. and the Staff Manual respectively. Title pages will be prepared in manuscript.

| Place | Date | Hour | Summary of Events and Information | Remarks and references to Appendices |
|---|---|---|---|---|
| ETAPLES | 12/1/19 | | Church services. Orders for advance party to DUNKIRK. | |
| | 13/1/19 | | 1 hours Iveaving, instructing, arrangement. Orders to move to DUNKIRK | |
| | 14/1/19 | | Entrained at ETAPLES & moved out at 11am. Bn. spent night in train on Dock Siding | |
| DUNKIRK | 15/1/19 | | Detrained at 14.30 hrs. Under canvas at MARDYCK. Bn. now 718 L.T. Bn. for administration | |
| | 16/1/19 | | 2/Lt R.V. MOORE M.C. from leave UK | |
| | | | Coys. put on detachment as follows. "D" to 36 Northumberland Fusiliers | |
| | | | "B" - 11 Royal Scots | |
| | | | "C" - 13 West Riding Regt. | |
| | 17/1/19 | | 'A' Co., H.Q., Q.M. + "E" erect + occupy rest canvas camp at MARDYCK. | |
| | | | 'A' Co. + H.Q. Cleaning up. B.C.D. work on demobilization camps | |
| | 18/1/19 | | 'A' Co. + H.Q. 1hr Ivy. + recreational games | |
| | 19/1/19 | | Church services. Capt PEARSON to UK on leave | |
| | 20/1/19 | | 'A' Co. to assist clearing up in A and B demob. camps/ | |
| | | | Capt F.H.D. HEAUME } from leave UK. | |
| | | | Capt S.C. HALL } | |
| | 21/1/19 | | 1 hrs manual + recreational games | |
| | 22/1/19 | | 2/Lt H.D. SETTLE to leave UK | |
| | 23/1/19 | | 2/Lt STOR. from A.G. to 11/R 2 S.F. to take over batts. | |
| | 24/1/19 | | Lt J.L. HUTCHISON M.C. to UK, demobilised | |
| | 25/1/19 | | 2/Lt E.C. HEPWORTH to leave UK. | |

Army Form C. 2118.

# WAR DIARY
## or
## INTELLIGENCE SUMMARY.
(Erase heading not required.)

Instructions regarding War Diaries and Intelligence
Summaries are contained in F. S. Regs., Part II.
and the Staff Manual respectively. Title pages
will be prepared in manuscript.

| Place | Date | Hour | Summary of Events and Information | Remarks and references to Appendices |
|---|---|---|---|---|
| DUNKIRK | 26/1/19 | | Working Parties measuring of R.E.S | |
| " | 27/1/19 | | do | |
| " | 28/1/19 | | do | |
| " | 29/1/19 | | do | |
| " | 30/1/19 | | do | |
| " | 31/1/19 | | do | |

R.M Andrews
Major
Commdg. 2/15th London Regt.

(6392) Wt. W6192/P875 1,500,000 4/18 McA & W Ltd (E 2815) Forms W3091/4.     Army Form W.3091.

# Cover for Documents.

2/15th BATTALION LONDON REGIMENT
**Nature of Enclosures.**

W A R    D I A R Y

for the month of FEBRUARY

*C.W.Gage.*
Lieut.-Colonel.

*2/15th Battalion London Regiment,*
*(P.W.O., Civil Service Rifles.)*

---

Notes, or Letters written.

Army Form C. 2118.

# WAR DIARY
## or
## INTELLIGENCE SUMMARY.
(Erase heading not required.)

Instructions regarding War Diaries and Intelligence Summaries are contained in F. S. Regs., Part II. and the Staff Manual respectively. Title pages will be prepared in manuscript.

| Place | Date | Hour | Summary of Events and Information | Remarks and references to Appendices |
|---|---|---|---|---|
| DUNKIRK | 1/2/19 | | 2ⁿᵈ LT A E ROBINSON alone behind | |
| " | 2/2/19 | | Orders received to arrange funeral and to arrange for Lt E's cock to take final roll call. BASE COMMANDANT appointed that become GENERAL PUKIRO LIEU 2ⁿᵈ LT M CHILD'S admittance | |
| " | 3/2/19 | | R.C.'D. Coy's took over duties under BASE COMMANDANT in view of Lt E's work at PETIT SYNTHE | |
| " | 4/2/19 | | Base duties | |
| " | 5/2/19 | | Base duties | |
| " | 6/2/19 | | LT T H E CLARK O.B.E. for demobilization | |
| " | 7/2/19 | | CAPT. F.W. LEWIS M.C. returned on U.K. for demobilization leave off strength | |
| " | 8/2/19 | | 2ⁿᵈ LT R.C. COOKE rejoined from leave. LT W.B. HOSTE M.C., LT W. EDWARDS, 2ⁿᵈ LT N. BROOKS, P. EWEN, H. KING and 123 other ranks proceed from 1ˢᵗ Base (Non combatants Corps) for Demob'y Centre. 2ⁿᵈ LT W.J. MURRAY returned to U.K | |
| " | 9/2/19 | | Base duties | |
| " | 10/2/19 | | 2ⁿᵈ LT J. MACMAHON D.C.M, M.M. evacuated to U.K | |

Army Form C. 2118.

# WAR DIARY
## or
## INTELLIGENCE SUMMARY.
(Erase heading not required.)

Instructions regarding War Diaries and Intelligence Summaries are contained in F. S. Regs., Part II. and the Staff Manual respectively. Title pages will be prepared in manuscript.

| Place | Date | Hour | Summary of Events and Information | Remarks and references to Appendices |
|---|---|---|---|---|
| DUNKIRK | 11/2/19 | | 2ⁿᵈ LT E.C. HEPWORTH rejoined from leave | PM |
| " | 12/2/19 | | 2ⁿᵈ LT R JACKSON to UK for demobilization. MAJOR R.B.W.G ANDREW, M.C. and CAPTAIN A. JOSLIN to UK on leave. | PM |
| " | 13/2/19 | | Base details. N.C. O's CLASS formed. | PM |
| " | 14/2/19 | | 2ⁿᵈ LT W.C. NICOLLS to UK for demobilization | PM |
| " | 15/2/19 | | Base details | PM |
| " | 16/2/19 | | " " | PM |
| " | 17/2/19 | | 2ⁿᵈ LT A.H. STEPHENS to U.K. for demob. | SMS |
| " | 18/2/19 | | Base details | PM |
| " | 19/2/19 | | 2ⁿᵈ LT P.H. CHUDLEY, 2ⁿᵈ LT L. MANTELL and 2ⁿᵈ LT F. RICHARDSON arrived 179 O/Rks joined from 34ᵗʰ LON REGT (RRR) - Non describable men | |
| " | 20/2/19 | | LT H.E. HOST to hospital. LT COL A.W. GAZE M.C. rejoined from 90ᵗʰ Bde 2ⁿᵈ LT H. BROOKS detached as member of F.G.C.M | SMS |
| " | 21/2/19 | | LT COL A.W. GAZE M.C. to hospital | SMS |
| " | 22/2/19 | | Base details etc. | PM |

Army Form C. 2118.

# WAR DIARY
## or
## INTELLIGENCE SUMMARY.
(Erase heading not required.)

Instructions regarding War Diaries and Intelligence Summaries are contained in F. S. Regs., Part II. and the Staff Manual respectively. Title pages will be prepared in manuscript.

| Place | Date | Hour | Summary of Events and Information | Remarks and references to Appendices |
|---|---|---|---|---|
| DUNKIRK | 23/2/19 | | Lt H E HOSTE, M.C. evacuated to U.K. | |
| " | 24/2/19 | | Lt Col A W GAZE M.C. rejoined from Hospital | |
| " | 25/2/19 | | Band concert | |
| " | 26/2/19 | | Lt J H WHEATLEY M.M. to U.K. then Lt A W BURCH rejoined from Leave | |
| " | 27/2/19 | | Lt F M CHUDLEY detailed as member of F.G.C.M. | |
| " | 28/2/19 | | Sgt C G.A CROSS 530810 awarded Medaille Militaire S.I. Evacuated 2 Hors (Sick) | |
| " | | | Band concert | |

A W Gaze Lt Col
2/15th Battalion London Regiment,
(P.W.O. Civil Service Rifles.)

2/15 London Regiment.

War Diary.

for

March 1919.

# WAR DIARY
## or
## INTELLIGENCE SUMMARY.
(Erase heading not required.)

Army Form C. 2118.

| Place | Date | Hour | Summary of Events and Information | Remarks and references to Appendices |
|---|---|---|---|---|
| DUNKIRK | 1/3/19 | | Lt. H.D. SETTLE to U.K. for demobilization. Instructions received from Base that Lieuts. should be relieved of duties by C.O. who could, if required, send Regt. on leave on arrival. | |
| " | 2/3/19 | | CAPT G.H. HETLEY M.C., LT. R.A. BRADFORD L.T. A.S. HILLS, LT. A.R. CHESTERTON, M.S. and 2nd LT. D.A.S. MANSING joined for duty from the 7th Lon Regt. Regtl. numbr. 148 9R.; CAPT. G.H. EDWARDS M.S. 2nd LT. G.G. BENNETT, 2nd LTs. C.Y. AULTLEY, 2nd LT. P.S. KIMPTON, 3/3/19 1/9 9Rs joined for duty from 3rd LON REGT | S.N |
| " | 3/3/19 | | 17th BATT ROYAL SUSSEX REGT commenced relief of Batt. | 1729 |
| " | 4/3/19 | | Batt. moved to PONT DE PETITE SYNTHE and occupied the following Loc/s. H.Qrs. No.10 Chemin Camp. A Coy No.13 Lucionline Camp. B & C Coys No.7 Chemin Camp and D Coy No.7 Chemin Camp. | |
| | | | CAPT. E.C. HALL, 2nd LT. T.H. IS CLARK and 2nd LT. J.O. YOS. R.Q.M.S. HARMAN 17/6ed and appointed of C.M.S., R.E.E. ceased 6/11/18 On leave of absence for civil employment to France pg. no 30/12/18. | M.3 |

# WAR DIARY
## or
## INTELLIGENCE SUMMARY.
*(Erase heading not required.)*

Army Form C. 2118.

Instructions regarding War Diaries and Intelligence Summaries are contained in F. S. Regs., Part II. and the Staff Manual respectively. Title pages will be prepared in manuscript.

| Place | Date | Hour | Summary of Events and Information | Remarks and references to Appendices |
|---|---|---|---|---|
| DUNKIRK | 5/7/19 | | Board of Enquiry to enquire into loss of Sergeant ... | |
| | | | S. RIVEY. PRESIDENT CAPT. A. WHITTING M.C. ... "R.E.s. | |
| | | | HEPWORTH and 2nd LT. L.M. ANTILL | |
| | | | Gunner No. 230098 SGT J.M. GALLAWAY, 230485 S.M. H.G. TUBB ... | (22) |
| | | | 530840 PTE P.H. VERNON awarded MILITARY MEDAL. 2nd LT A.P. PITAM | |
| | | | M.C. to U.K. Leave 2nd LT H BROOKS to England | |
| | 6/3/19 | | Advance party of 5 officers and 25 o.r.s. left for ETAPLES ... | |
| | | | ... | |
| | 7/3/19 | | CAPT. B. PEATFIELD M.C. to be C/MAJOR & ... | |
| | | | ... L/A/CAPT R.B.W.G. ANDREW M.C. to be A/MAJOR | (22) |
| | | | ... 21.3.19 | |
| | | | 16.2.19 A.G. S/37797 ... | |
| | 8/3/19 | | MAJOR ANDREW M.C. and CAPT. A. JOSLIN ... | |
| | 9/3/19 | | Relief of ... by 1st ... | |
| | 10/3/19 | | 2nd LT D.A. MANNING to U.K. on ... | (22) |
| | 11/3/19 | | LT. R.A. BRADFORD M.C. to U.K. ... | |

# WAR DIARY
## or
## INTELLIGENCE SUMMARY.
(Erase heading not required.)

Army Form C. 2118.

Instructions regarding War Diaries and Intelligence Summaries are contained in F. S. Regs., Part II. and the Staff Manual respectively. Title pages will be prepared in manuscript.

| Place | Date | Hour | Summary of Events and Information | Remarks and references to Appendices |
|---|---|---|---|---|
| DUNKIRK | 11/3/19 | | At 11.00 hrs. empl. awoke all DANNES CAMIERS STATION at 22.00 hrs. Whole command under canvas sight. | 3/19 |
| DANNES | 12/3/19 | | Batt. arrived at 03.00 hrs. Regt. were en-trained & billeted A Coy to NEUFCHATEL, B Coy to DANNES H.Qrs. C & D Coys to ST CECILS PLAGE. A & B Coys took over the guards of DANNES AMMUNITION DUMP. C & D coys training. S.O.C. DIV. under orders & inspected camp. | S.M. |
| ST CECILS PLAGE | 13/3/19 | | C & D Coys training. 2 Lts. D.A. GODDARD & R.M. WILLIAMS D.C.M. joined from U.K. base. | S.M. |
| " | 14/3/19 | | Training | S.M. |
| " | 15/3/19 | | Training | S.M. |
| " | 16/3/19 | | Church Parade at 10.30 hrs. | S.M. |
| " | 17/3/19 | | Training. G.O.C. DIV. visited Camp & inspected Camp. 2 Lt. T.R. EWEN and Lt. W. COHEN to Report. | S.M. |
| " | 18/3/19 | | Training. G.O.C. DIV. inspected guards furn. by A & B Coys at DANNES AMMUNITION DUMP. Drafted 2 Offrs. CAPT W. OFFLER CAPT G. PRINCE & 1 O.R. ENGLEBACH together with 98 O.R. further 2 Lt. A.R. CHESTERTON M.C. to U.K. Revd. 1/13 LON REGT. | S.M. |

Army Form C. 2118.

# WAR DIARY
## or
## INTELLIGENCE SUMMARY.
(Erase heading not required.)

Instructions regarding War Diaries and Intelligence Summaries are contained in F. S. Regs., Part II. and the Staff Manual respectively. Title pages will be prepared in manuscript.

| Place | Date | Hour | Summary of Events and Information | Remarks and references to Appendices |
|---|---|---|---|---|
| ST CECILE PLAGE | 19/3/19 | | Training. Men worked up on shore near CASINO HOTEL, ST CECILE PLAGE. 1/Lt W.G. PAINE, 2nd Lt J.T. ENGLEBACK and 98 O.R. joined Batt. from 1/3rd LON REGT. C + D coys Rest Rets Carts. | SUN |
| - // - | 20/3/19 | | Training | MON |
| - // - | 21/3/19 | | Training | TUES |
| - // - | 22/3/19 | | Lt SYMON, H.T.B. joined Batt. from 3rd LON REGT. The Brigadier watched Comps. C + D coys Rest Rets Carts | WED |
| - // - | 23/3/19 | | Stand Down. | THURS |
| - // - | 24/3/19 | | Training. Hot Baths for Everyone off N Coy. | FRI |
| - // - | 25/3/19 | | Training. The Brigadier inspected A Coy at work. Lt H. & S. SIMON 2 UK Leave | SAT |
| - // - | 26/3/19 | | Training. MAJOR R.W.G.ANDREW, M.C. PRESIDENT of ROUEN ETAPLES | SUN |
| - // - | 27/3/19 | | Training 2/Lt D.A.S. MANNING from UK Leave | MON |
| - // - | 28/3/19 | | Training. 2/Lt A.P. PITTAIN, MC from UK Leave. Orders received for the 29 Bn to take over Regnal area on 1 | TUES |

B. D. & I., London, E.C.
Wt W1771/M2931 750,000 5/17 Sch. 52 Forms/C.2118/14
(A8204)

**Army Form C. 2118.**

# WAR DIARY
or
## INTELLIGENCE SUMMARY.
(Erase heading not required.)

Instructions regarding War Diaries and Intelligence Summaries are contained in F. S. Regs., Part II. and the Staff Manual respectively. Title pages will be prepared in manuscript.

| Place | Date | Hour | Summary of Events and Information | Remarks and references to Appendices |
|---|---|---|---|---|
| ST CECILE PLAGE | 29/1/19 | | C & D coys moved to BOULOGNE AREA. Both coys to stay at N° 63 REST CAMP. Offrs the night 29/30. G about 30 O.R. Coy's have also 2/Lt W. BERKS REGT on P.O.W. Guard, numbers to be made up 89 O.R. | |
| " | 30/1/19 | | Weather fine. C Coy to be drawn 30 Labour Group N° 2 then RIVILLE and D Coy to Etaples 6 Labour Group to Le OUTREAUX | |
| " | 31/1/19 | | L.V. S. BURT C. R. for standing. | |

adj & Lt. Col.
Commanding.

*[stamp: 15th Battalion London Regiment (P.W.O. Civil Service Rifles)]*

War Diary.

2/15 London Regiment.

April 1919.

J. B. Follett Lt. Col.
Commanding
2/15th Battalion London Regiment,
(P.W.O. Civil Service Rifles.)

# WAR DIARY
## or
## INTELLIGENCE SUMMARY.

*(Erase heading not required.)*

Army Form C. 2118.

| Place | Date | Hour | Summary of Events and Information | Remarks and references to Appendices |
|---|---|---|---|---|
| St Cecile Plage | 1-4-19 2-4-19 | | 2nd Lt J H Wheatley MM posted to 9th London Regt | AKC |
| " " | 3-4-19 | | Capt G H Hetley MC proceeded to UK on 14 days leave. | AKC |
| " " | 4-4-19 | 12.30 pm | BRIGADIER visited HQ's | AKC |
| " " | 5-4-19 6-4-19 7-4-19 | | 2nd Lt A K Chatterton MC returned from 14 days leave in U.K. Voluntary Church Services 2/Lt J G Hills } proceeded on 14 days leave to U.K. 2/Lt P F Knapton } | AKC AKC AKC |
| " " | 8-4-19 9-4-19 10-4-19 | | 2/Lt R V Moon MC to U.K. for Duty Benefit" Capt H A Taylor M.C. to PARIS leave Lt. Simson returned from U.K. leave. | AKC AKC AKC |
| " " | 11.4.19 | | Capt. S.C. HALL & Capt. T.H. Du HEAUME to PARIS leave. Three (3) mines previously washed up on beach at St. CECIL PLAGE, were exploded by Lieut Frue by French Authorities. | AKC |
| " " | 12.4.19 13.4.19 | | Lt W.G. PAINE to U.K. leave. 2 NCO's and 6 men returned to BHQ from 154 P.O.W. Coy. Lt. J.B. Simson assumes command of "B" Coy, vice Lt W.G. PAINE to U.K. leave. Notification received that T.W. PEARSON & 2/Lt. K.P. NEALL retained in UK for early demob. Capt Pearson W.O.O. 17.2.19. 2/Lt. K.P. Neall " 30.1.19. | AKC |
| " " | 14.4.19 | | 2/Lt HUTLEY rejoined from UK leave. Lt W.G. PAINE to U.K. leave. | AKC |
| " " | 15.4.19 | | | AKC |

Army Form C. 2118.

# WAR DIARY
## or
## INTELLIGENCE SUMMARY.
*(Erase heading not required.)*

Instructions regarding War Diaries and Intelligence Summaries are contained in F. S. Regs., Part II. and the Staff Manual respectively. Title pages will be prepared in manuscript.

| Place | Date | Hour | Summary of Events and Information | Remarks and references to Appendices |
|---|---|---|---|---|
| ST.CECIL PLAGE. | 16.4.19 | | 2/Lt. E.J.MINNS to U.K. leave. Draft of 4 Officers & 39 O.R. joined from 1/5th London. Officers {2/Lt. C.E.BARNETT. M.C. 2/Lt. W.J.BURCHETT. 2/Lt. J.W.HALIFAX. 2/Lt. B.W.PRYNN. C Coy. returned to B.H.Q. at ST.CECIL PLAGE having been relieved at BOULOGNE. 2/Lt. W.G.BENNETT 2/Lt. G.L.BONNER } from U.K. leave. 2/Lt. ENGLEBACK | A/1158 |
| " | 17.4.19 | | BRIGADIER visits BHQ. | A/1159 |
| " | 18.4.19 | | Good Friday — Voluntary Church Services Capt. S.C. HALL from PARIS leave Capt. F.H.Du HEAUME " " U.K. leave Capt. ASTLEY " " U.K. leave | A/1158 |
| " | 19.4.19 | | Army | A/1158 |
| " | 20.4.19 | | EASTER SUNDAY. Voluntary Church Parade. C.O. inspects C and H.Q. Coys. | |
| " | 21.4.19 | | 2/Lt. A.G. LANDER to U.K. leave. Capt. A.H. JOSLIN from U.K. special leave. Lt. COLONEL FOLLITT (WARWICKSHIRE Rgt) posted 1st BATT'N. | |
| " | 22.4.19 | | C Coy. move to ETAPLES to be quartered in M.M. Camp, and take over duties from 1/6t CHESHIRES AT No. 26 GENERAL HOSPITAL ETAPLES No. 51 Lt. A.G. ORDE from U.K. leave | |
| " | 23.4.19 | | Capt. G.H. Hetley M.C. to Special French leave. Lt.Col. A.W. Gaye M.C. 2/Lt. C.B. Engush 2/Lt. A.P. Pitam M.C. } To U.K. for demob'n | |
| " | 24.4.19 | | Lt. Col. C.B. Follett DSO. M.C. (Royal Warwickshire Rgt.) assumes Command of Battalion. | A/1158 |

# WAR DIARY
## or
## INTELLIGENCE SUMMARY.

*(Erase heading not required.)*

Army Form C. 2118.

| Place | Date | Hour | Summary of Events and Information | Remarks and references to Appendices |
|---|---|---|---|---|
| Ste. Cecile Plage | 24.4.19 | | Brigadier visits B.H.Q. | A168 |
| " | 25.4.19 | | 2/Lt. P.F. Kington from U.K. leave. | A168 |
| " | 27.4.19 | | Lt. N.A. Dayton. M.C. (Arc. U.S.A) appointed Captain Authority Special Order No. 48 Amer. E.Y.P. Force. | A168 |
| " | 28.4.19 | | Capt. B. Stoketley M.C. rejoined from Special Trench Leave. | |
| " | 26.4.19 | | Lt. Col. A. Wayte. D.S.O. (Sherwood Forester) reported for duty | A168 |
| " | 29.4.19 | | Capt. N.A. Dayton. M.C. (ARC. USA) rejoined from Paris leave. | A168 |
| " | 30.4.19 | | Capt. G.H. Edwards M.C. from U.K. sick leave. Lt. Col. A. Wayte D.S.O. left Battalion to take command of 13 Bttn Duke of Wellington's own (West Yorks Regt.) | A168 |

J. G. Follett. D. Col.
2/15th Battalion London Regiment.
(P.W.O. Civil Service Rifles.)

2/15 London Regiment.

War Diary.
for
May 1919.

                    Lt Col.
              Commanding.
2/15th Battalion London Regiment.
(P.W.O. Civil Service Rifles.)

# WAR DIARY
## or
## INTELLIGENCE SUMMARY.

*(Erase heading not required.)*

Army Form C. 2118.

Instructions regarding War Diaries and Intelligence Summaries are contained in F. S. Regs., Part II. and the Staff Manual respectively. Title pages will be prepared in manuscript.

| Place | Date | Hour | Summary of Events and Information | Remarks and references to Appendices |
|---|---|---|---|---|
| ST CECILE PLAGE | 1/5/19 | | CAPT F H DU HIEAUME granted special leave to BETHUNE | SMc |
| | 2/5/19 | | Notification received that LT H. DU HIEAUME relinquishes Acting rank of CAPT whilst commanding Company (Authy. hor ord. N6234 dated 6/4/19). | SMc |
| | 3/5/19 | | P.G.C.M. Convilled at No.1 to 20 of 10 CECILE PLAGE for trial of PTE FLANDERS. T.M. Officers (Convening O.R.) also attached LT. L.G. BENNETT. CAPT F. H. DU HIEAUME returned from special leave to BETHUNE | SMc |
| | 4/5/19 | | LT W.G. MAINS returned from U.K. leave. Voluntary Church Service | SMc |
| | 5/5/19 | | Return of arms & blankets to Ordnance. | SMc |
| | 5/5/19 | | Supplementary working parties to Lry. 2nd LT J. JOHNSON, A.S. O'NEILL and O.C. A STAPLES joined party for duty. from R.W.K.R. | SMc |
| | 5/5/19 | | G.O.C. DIVISION inspected Guards Divisional Dump. LT H.A. BANKS (6th Chester Regt) and 2/LT R.H RIANT (A3" LON Regt) joined Bn for duty. 2 LT J MIALL reported from U.K. leave | SMc |
| | 5/5/19 | | C O visited D COY at BOULOGNE. CAPT S.C. HALL to U.K. leave | SMc |
| | 9/5/19 | | C O attended Conference at Base re: Rail Etaples. HEPWORTH to U.K. for discharge | SMc |
| | 10/5/19 | | Front Column arrived with Coy & Bn HQ on R. Camp R Coy reported. Coy HQ on R Camp from Hapleyne | SMc |

D. D. & L., London, E.C.
(A8-24) Wt W.7771/M2031 730,000 5/17 **Sch. 52** Forms/C2118/14

Army Form C. 2118.

# WAR DIARY
## or
## INTELLIGENCE SUMMARY.
(Erase heading not required.)

Instructions regarding War Diaries and Intelligence Summaries are contained in F. S. Regs., Part II. and the Staff Manual respectively. Title pages will be prepared in manuscript.

| Place | Date | Hour | Summary of Events and Information | Remarks and references to Appendices |
|---|---|---|---|---|
| ST CLBERT PLACE | 11/3/19 | | 2/LT P. DRAPER reports for duty. Compulsory Church Parade. Special Order of the Day by B.G.O.C. Read. Troops in Square uncovered. | P28 |
| | 12/3/19 | | D Coy Training. | R.M. |
| | 13/3/19 | | Training | R.M. |
| | 14/3/19 | | 2/LT P.R. KIMPTON to Course at BERKHAMSTEAD | R.M. |
| | 15/3/19 | | 2/LT R.H. RIANT admitted to NO.4 GEN HOSP | R.M. |
| | 16/3/19 | | 2/LT F.R. RICHARDS proceeds to U.K. on leave. | R.M. |
| | 17/3/19 | | D Coys & H.Q. & S Coy Rec Rel Baths | R.M. |
| | 18/3/19 | | Voluntary Church Parade | R.M. |
| | 19/3/19 | | 2/LT J.W. HALLIDAY to U.K. for leave. CAPT A.E. MONTAGUE (R.E.) joins for duty | R.M. |
| | 20/3/19 | | LT & Q.M J. HAWKINS (12 NORFOLKS) proceeds for duty. Orders received for Batt to move to ABBEVILLE | R.M. |
| | 21/3/19 | | ADVANCE PARTY TO ABBEVILLE | R.M. |

Army Form C. 2118.

# WAR DIARY
## or
## INTELLIGENCE SUMMARY.
(Erase heading not required.)

Instructions regarding War Diaries and Intelligence
Summaries are contained in F. S. Regs., Part II.
and the Staff Manual respectively. Title pages
will be prepared in manuscript.

| Place | Date | Hour | Summary of Events and Information | Remarks and references to Appendices |
|---|---|---|---|---|
| ST CECILE PLAGE | 22/5/19 | | Bast entrained at ETAPLES for ABBEVILLE at 1400 hrs and arrived at ABBEVILLE at 1640hrs. Transit marched to SIGNALS DEPOT & remained there for the night | |
| ABBEVILLE | 23/5/19 | | Orders received for Batt to supply guards to W. Gents & to relieve 3/5 Batt GLOUCESTERS and 11 BATT EAST LANCS. Batt assigned as follows: HdQrs H2 & B COYS at ST RIQUIER, A & D COYS ABBEVILLE, B COY SAIGNIVILLE and C COY PRESSANVILLE | 8.11. |
| ST RIQUIER | 24/5/19 | | CAPT SC HALL rejoined from UK leave | 5.11. |
| " | 25/5/19 | | Voluntary Church Parade | 8.11. |
| " | 26/5/19 | | Bare platoon A coy + D coy training | 8.11. |
| " | 27/5/19 | | A coy 7th Pln moved to VAUCHELLES for duty. 2/LT G.W. PRYNN to A.P.M. ABBEVILLE | 8.11. |
| " | 28/5/19 | | 2/ LT G.W. PRYNN to UK leave. LT F.M. CHUDLEY to A.P.M. ABBEVILLE to relieve 2/LT PRYNN | 8.11. |
| " | 29/5/19 | | Bart 7K Pln moved to VAUCHELLES. 2/LT M ANTILL to U K leave | 8.11. |
| " | 30/5/19 | | O C Dir visits Posts at 2a. 2/LT O'NEILL to U K leave | 8.11. |
| " | 31/5/19 | | D. coy moves from ABBEVILLE to 9 C ROW coy near VAUCHELLES | 7.11. |

F W Smith Lt Col
2/15th Battalion London Regiment,
(P.W.O. Civil Service Rifles.)

(6414) Wt. W3906/P1607 2,500,000 7/18 McA & W Ltd (E 3591) Forms W3091/4.     Army Form W.3091.

# Cover for Documents.

Nature of Enclosures.

2/15th London Regiment.

War Diary.

for

June 1919

Notes, or Letters written.

2/15th Battalion London Regiment,
(P.W.O. Civil Service Rifles.)

Army Form C. 2118.

# WAR DIARY
## or
## INTELLIGENCE SUMMARY.
(Erase heading not required.)

Instructions regarding War Diaries and Intelligence Summaries are contained in F. S. Regs., Part II. and the Staff Manual respectively. Title pages will be prepared in manuscript.

| Place | Date | Hour | Summary of Events and Information | Remarks and references to Appendices |
|---|---|---|---|---|
| VAUCHELLES | 1/6/19 | | 2/Lt E.J. Mill to U.K. for demob. Major N.J. Tortise, D.S.O. 7/Y. Regt. was today appt. gained for camp. G.O.C. arrived back to 2/o 2/Lt F.R. Richards from U.K. leave | 9am |
| " | 2/6/19 | | 2/Lt D.A. Manning, M.C. to H.Q's 16" Bdr. Bgt Staples for General Comas | 8am |
| " | 3/6/19 | | Capt A.A. Joslin to U.K. for demob. Court of Enquiry Reconvened at 2p to Enquire into report of charm rehort Convey of 9/5/19. | 9am |
| " | 4/6/19 | | Lt W.G. Paine to U.K. for demob. and Lt A.G. Wills | 9am |
| " | 5/6/19 | | Capt F.H. Du Heaume to U.K. for demob. Capt N.A. Dayton, M.C. A.P.C. U.S.A. attached to no 2 Military Hosp. for duty. | 8pm |
| " | 6/6/19 | | Capt Coatsworth R.A.M.C. attached for duty to No. 6 (Working) U.S. coy.) | 9am |
| " | 7/6/19 | | Raining. | 9am |
| " | 8/6/19 | | Whit Sunday. Voluntary Church Service. | 9pm |
| " | 9/6/19 | | Fine fine warm day. Held at Abbeville Garrison Sports | 9pm |

Army Form C. 2118.

# WAR DIARY
## or
## INTELLIGENCE SUMMARY.
(Erase heading not required.)

Instructions regarding War Diaries and Intelligence Summaries are contained in F. S. Regs., Part II. and the Staff Manual respectively. Title pages will be prepared in manuscript.

| Place | Date | Hour | Summary of Events and Information | Remarks and references to Appendices |
|---|---|---|---|---|
| VAUCHELLES | 10/6/19 | | Training & Educational work. MAJOR R B W G ANDREW M C to STAPLES to Hospital T R G C M | A11 |
| " " | 11/6/19 | | Training | A11 |
| " " | 12/6/19 | | " " MAJOR H J TORTISE D S O assumed command of Regiment in absence of rest. | A11 |
| " " | 13/6/19 | | Training 2/LT G W PAYNE from U R Camp attached to A/M A BOSQUE 2/LT H MANTLE from U R Camp Lt T H CHURLEY rejoins unit | A11 |
| " " | 14/6/19 | | Training & Educational work. | A11 |
| " " | 15/6/19 | | MAJOR R B W G ANDREW M C & 2/LT J U R for dental treatment. LT COL P B FOLLETT D S O M E to U R Camp Voluntary Courses Training | A11 |
| " " | 16/6/19 | | MAJOR H J TORTISE D S O again assumes command of Regt | A11 |
| " " | 17/6/19 | | Training & Educational work 2/LT A G O'NEILL rejoins from U R Camp | A11 |
| " " | 18/6/19 | | 2/LT J JOHNSON to Hospital | F11 |
| " " | 19/6/19 | | LT F B SIMON rejoined from D A G H Q & 2/LT A G STAPLES rejoined to Hospital | F11 |

# WAR DIARY
## or
## INTELLIGENCE SUMMARY.

Army Form C. 2118.

(Erase heading not required.)

| Place | Date | Hour | Summary of Events and Information | Remarks and references to Appendices |
|---|---|---|---|---|
| VAUCHELLES | 20/9/19 | | Bomb & Bayonet practice all B Coy & C Coy D Coy's to engines nets (be assembled) made out of the RIFLES belonging to N.B. 6483 Pte NEWTON and taken to provost when unreported by took place for the coy frames | App A |
| " | 21/9/19 | | Company Training work | App B |
| " | 22/9/19 | | 22 Lewis Gun classes | App C |
| " | 23/9/19 | | 2/Lt LEWIS OT Wheeler 2 L O/A detailed to A.D.M. ABBEVILLE for escort C coy and one party Some with ? MOTOR AMB. TRPT. Lt BRADFORD and Lt H A BANCHI & U.R. proceeding | App D |
| " | 24/9/19 | | 2/Lt A G O'NEILL to hospital. 2 Lt DAWTREY to WAIL 2/Lt Railway Resc Camps. Lt P N. CRUDLEY to Pont L/Cpl MANNING H C | App E |
| " | 25/9/19 | | 2/Lt ENGLEBACH to Course at ETAPLES operation from Somme | App F |
| " | 26/9/19 | | Training, Cerematory work | App G |
| " | 27/9/19 | | Training, Ceremonial work | App H |
| " | 28/9/19 | | — | App J |
| " | 29/9/19 | | | App K |

Army Form C. 2118.

# WAR DIARY
## or
## INTELLIGENCE SUMMARY.
(Erase heading not required.)

Instructions regarding War Diaries and Intelligence Summaries are contained in F. S. Regs., Part II. and the Staff Manual respectively. Title pages will be prepared in manuscript.

2/16th Battalion London Regiment,
(P.W.O. Civil Service Rifles.)

| Place | Date | Hour | Summary of Events and Information | Remarks and references to Appendices |
|---|---|---|---|---|
| WAVENDEN | 30/6/19 | | REU R EDWARDS to U.K. leave. | |

2/16TH BATTN. LONDON REGIMENT
No.
30 JUN. 1919
(P.W.O. CIVIL SERVICE RIFLES)

(6414) Wt. W3906/P1607 2,500,000  7/18  McA & W Ltd  (E 3591)  Forms W3091/4.  Army Form W.3091.

# Cover for Documents.

### Nature of Enclosures.

War Diary

for

July 1919.

2/15th London Regiment.

Notes, or Letters written.

L. B. Lublt
D Col
6org
2/15th Battalion London Regiment,
(P.W.O. Civil Service Rifles.)

# WAR DIARY
## or
## INTELLIGENCE SUMMARY.

Army Form C. 2118.

| Place | Date | Hour | Summary of Events and Information | Remarks and references to Appendices |
|---|---|---|---|---|
| VAUCHELLES | 1/7/19 | | Revue Review held in ABBEVILLE in conjunction with French CAPT G.H. HITLEY M.C. and 100 other officers & 100 other ranks attended. CAPT S.C. HALE acted as Captain to the O.C. W WHYTE D.S.O.M.C. who was in charge of representation from the 30th Bde. | P/O |
| " | 2/7/19 | | Bn Commander inspected Coys A, B, C, & D Coys training, musketry, firing, guards, P.O.W. escorts, & completion of each | P/O |
| " | 3/7/19 | | Training & Equipment work | P/O |
| " | 4/7/19 | | " " Lt W.T. BORCHETT to U.K. leave | P/O |
| " | 5/7/19 | | " " | P/O |
| " | 6/7/19 | | Coventry Church Services | P/O |
| " | 7/7/19 | | Regular general inspected Bays & R.E. One platoon of each Coy Training & Command work, manoeuvre firing, guards, POW escort. | P/O |
| " | 8/7/19 | | Training as per above. Lt Col F.B. FOLLETT D.S.O. M.C. reported from U.K. leave. | P/O |

# WAR DIARY
## or
## INTELLIGENCE SUMMARY.
*(Erase heading not required.)*

Army Form C. 2118.

| Place | Date | Hour | Summary of Events and Information | Remarks and references to Appendices |
|---|---|---|---|---|
| VAUCHELLES | 9/7/19 | | Training as per plan | DR |
| " | 10/7/19 | | " " | DR |
| " | 11/7/19 | | RSM McFarlane H.L.I. proceeds on leave to UK. Capt G.B.S. Montagu on draft leave to UK | DR |
| " | 12/7/19 | | Training as per plan Lt T.A. Goddard British Army | DR |
| " | 13/7/19 | | Resting about Vaucan | DR |
| " | 14/7/19 | | Church Parade | DR |
| " | 15/7/19 | | Training as per plan 2Lt P. Kingston reported from course at RETHEL HOSPRA R.O/C Bath Lon Regt returns 3 coy duty from OC VAUN | DR |
| " | 16/7/19 | | Training as per plan Capt H.E. Rae R2V.R. 12 Wards D.C.M reports from UK Lt R.R. Kindley reported from England | DR |
| " | 17/7/19 | | Training as per plan 2Lt J.H. Johnson reported from England 2Lt T. English Bach, CSM Boucheday reported from course at Cooper | DR |

Army Form C. 2118.

# WAR DIARY
## or
## INTELLIGENCE SUMMARY.
(Erase heading not required.)

Instructions regarding War Diaries and Intelligence Summaries are contained in F. S. Regs., Part II. and the Staff Manual respectively. Title pages will be prepared in manuscript.

| Place | Date | Hour | Summary of Events and Information | Remarks and references to Appendices |
|---|---|---|---|---|
| VAUCHELLES | 18/7/19 | | Training. Educational work | |
| " | 19/7/19 | | Public Holiday. Fêtes opened | |
| " | 20/7/19 | | Church Parade. 2/Lt W. Burchett reported from U.K. leave | |
| " | 21/7/19 | | Lt P. Draper to U.K. leave. C.S.M. Worley proceeded to STAPLES on course | |
| " | 22/7/19 | | Training & Educational work | |
| " | 23/7/19 | | do | |
| " | 24/7/19 | | do | |
| " | 25/7/19 | | Lt C.R. Barnett and Lt B. Manning, M.O. to U.K. leave. | |
| " | 26/7/19 | | do | |
| " | 27/7/19 | | do | |
| " | 27/7/19 | | Voluntary Church Service | |

(A8-04) D. D. & L. London, E.C. Wt W1771/M2031 750,000 5/17 Sch. 52 Forms/C2118/14

# WAR DIARY
## or
## INTELLIGENCE SUMMARY.

Army Form C. 2118.

(Erase heading not required.)

| Place | Date | Hour | Summary of Events and Information | Remarks and references to Appendices |
|---|---|---|---|---|
| VAUCHELLES | 1/5/19 | | Training - Educational Work | |
| — | 2/5/19 | | do | |
| — | 2/6/19 | | do | |
| — | 3/7/19 | | do | |

J. A. Follett Lt. Col.
2/18th Battalion London Regiment,
(P.W.O. Civil Service Rifles.)

1919.

SECRET.

WAR DIARY

OF THE

2/15TH. LONDON REGIMENT
(CIVIL SERVICE RIFLES.)

FOR THE MONTH OF AUGUST, 1919.

(VOLUME NO.      )

September 1st. 1919.

*[signature]* LIEUT. COLONEL.
Commanding 2/15TH. LONDON REGIMENT.(C.S.R.)

**WAR DIARY**
or
**INTELLIGENCE SUMMARY.**

Army Form C. 2118.

Instructions regarding War Diaries and Intelligence Summaries are contained in F. S. Regs., Part II. and the Staff Manual respectively. Title pages will be prepared in manuscript.

(Erase heading not required.)

| Place | Date | Hour | Summary of Events and Information | Remarks and references to Appendices |
|---|---|---|---|---|
| VAUXHALL | 14/8/19 | | Training - Generaduck work | |
| | 15/8/19 | | 2nd Lt C LANDER to U.K. on leave. Training as per above | |
| | 16/8/19 | | 2nd Lt J JOHNSON from U.K. leave. do | |
| | 17/8/19 | | Commanding Officer inspected C & D at GREENVILLE. Training as per above | |
| | 18/8/19 | | do | |
| | 19/8/19 | | Lt L P BENNETT to hospital | |
| | 20/8/19 | | Saturday - closed down | |
| | 21/8/19 | | Training as per above | |
| | | | 2nd Lt Lee to Egypt on leave. | |
| | | | Officer commanding the Bde of Cavalry lodged a formal complaint against 2nd Lt Y TORTLEY | |
| | | | 15th Hussars 14 INFANTRY 2nd IA GODDARD BRIGADE GENERAL visited 1st Bn | |
| | 28/8/19 | | Training as per above | |
| | 29/8/19 | | Training as per above | |
| | 30/8/19 | | do | |
| | 22/8/19 | | do | |
| | 23/8/19 | | do | |

# WAR DIARY or INTELLIGENCE SUMMARY

Army Form C. 2118.

| Place | Date | Hour | Summary of Events and Information | Remarks and references to Appendices |
|---|---|---|---|---|
| VAUCHELLES | 1/8/19 | | BN COMMANDER inspects BATT HQRS & Companies & thorn huts | |
| | 2/8/19 | | Lectures of each Coy. Training as per plan | |
| | 3/8/19 | | LT J A GODDARD rejoined from UK leave. 2/LT A K CHESTERTON to hospital. LT H G SIMON to hospital on Gallipoli. Training as per plan. Officers | |
| " | 4/8/19 | | Voluntary Church service | |
| " | 5/8/19 | | Bank Holiday. Training as per plan | |
| " | 6/8/19 | | LT G A TAPLEY DCM to UK on leave. LT G L BONNER to UK for course. Training as per plan | |
| " | 7/8/19 | | LT H CHUDLEY to hospital. Training as per plan | |
| " | 8/8/19 | | do do | |
| " | 9/8/19 | | do do | |
| " | 10/8/19 | | Voluntary Church service | |

# WAR DIARY

## INTELLIGENCE SUMMARY

Army Form C. 2118.

*(Erase heading not required.)*

| Place | Date | Hour | Summary of Events and Information | Remarks and references to Appendices |
|---|---|---|---|---|
| VAUCHELLES | 25/8/19 | | Training of Examiners Work | |
| | 26/8/19 | | do | |
| | 27/8/19 | | Returning third horses | |
| | 28/8/19 | | Training of Examiners Work. Orders issued to everybody who had given written attestation of wish to continue in service to be so reported to be in readiness before 04.00 tomorrow morning for departure to U.K. for demobilization. | |
| | 28/8/19 | | Examiners Work 34 | |
| | 28/8/19 | | do do — 31 | |
| | 29/8/19 | | do do — 34 | |
| | 29/8/19 | | do do — Capt. & adj. S.C. HALL to U.K. for demobilization. Lt. G.H. HETLEY to U.K. Records office to obtain full particulars of personnel. | |
| | 30/8/19 | | Training. N.C.O's class to LE TREPORT for day trip. | |
| | 31/8/19 | | Voluntary Church Service. | |

To Headquarters
Abbeville Sub-Area.

> HEADQUARTERS,
> ABBEVILLE AREA.
> No 73/D
> Date 14..10..19.

War Diary of this unit for the month of September herewith.

[signature]

Lieut. & Adjutant.
for O.C. 2/15th. London Regiment.
(P.W.O. Civil Service Rifles.)

> 2/15TH BATTALION,
> P.W.O. CIVIL
> SERVICE RIFLES.
> No. B/1769
> Date 13/10/19.

The Secretary
    War Office.(SD 2)
        LONDON.

-------------------------------

Sir,

    I beg to forward Herewith War Diary of this Battalion for the month of September 1919.

        I have the honour to be, Sir,
            Your obedient servant,

*Allan G O'Neill*
        Lieut.
   O.C. Equipment Guard.
2/15th. Battalion. London Regiment
  (P.W.O. Civil Service Rifles.)

18/10/19.

Army Form C. 2118.

# WAR DIARY
## or
## INTELLIGENCE SUMMARY.
(Erase heading not required.)

Instructions regarding War Diaries and Intelligence Summaries are contained in F.S. Regs., Part II. and the Staff Manual respectively. Title pages will be prepared in manuscript.

| Place | Date | Hour | Summary of Events and Information | Remarks and references to Appendices |
|---|---|---|---|---|
| Vaudelles | 1/9/19 | | Training as usual. Seven from 90th Bde & attached to 182 Bde at Mouts | See |
| — | 2/9/19 | | Training as usual. Eslin, near Dieppe | See |
| — | 3/9/19 | | Training as usual. G.O.C. 182 Bde called in afternoon & men | See |
| — | 4/9/19 | | proceeded to U.K. as demobilization | See |
| — | 5/9/19 | | Training as usual | |
| — | 6/9/19 | | Capt G.E. MONTAGUE to U.K. with instructions to report to W.O. Training as usual | See |
| — | | | L'/G.W. PRYNN to U.K. on special leave. Training as usual | See |
| — | 7/9/19 | | L'/G.H. WHITLEY returned from Reg'tl Office London | See |
| — | 8/9/19 | | Voluntary Church services. Training as usual. Bones Given to Ball'n in Altevelle | See |
| — | 9/9/19 | | Training as usual | See |
| — | 10/9/19 | | — L'/ PRYNN returned from special leave | See |
| — | 11/9/19 | | — 2L'/ C.V.D.R Whitley to U.K. on leave | See |
| — | 12/9/19 | | Weapons ittk DSO. Rivertice of Court Martial attached | See |

# WAR DIARY
## or
## INTELLIGENCE SUMMARY.
(Erase heading not required.)

Army Form C. 2118.

| Place | Date | Hour | Summary of Events and Information | Remarks and references to Appendices |
|---|---|---|---|---|
| Vaucheller | 13.9.19 | | Lt. A.K. CHESTERTON M.C. rejoined from hospital. MEDs closed to HETHERSETT. | Sm |
| | 14.9.19 | | Voluntary Church service. A.O. 321 reducing all Rentry + Valuations. | Sm |
| | | | Soldiers have received. | |
| | 15.9.19 | | B Company at SAIGNEVILLE and C Coy at FRETEMOUFFROY relieved by | |
| | | | 20th Bn HANTS Regt + proceeded to AUSTRALIA Hospital at ABBEVILLE | |
| | | | 2/Lt GODDARD + 2/Lt WILLIAMS DCM E.V.K. for | |
| | | | demobilization. Instruction that Battalion is any reverse to Cadre | |
| | | | received. | |
| | 16.9.19 | | 30 O.R. demobilized. | Sm |
| | | | 1 Officer + 13 O.R. on expanded front. | |
| | | | Dispersal of Canteen funds 6,000 (carried fwd) | Sm |
| | 17.9.19 | | 30 O.R. demobilized. | Sm |
| | 18.9.19 | | 30 O.R. —"— Bruce K. Goat in ABBEVILLE. | Sm |
| | 19.9.19 | | 30 O.R. —"— Coy Football began. | Sm |
| | 20.9.19 | | 2/Lt KIMPTON + 30 O.R. to Education Centre, Stanford Le SE. Football League | |
| | | | 30 O.R. demobilized. | Sm |
| | 21.9.19 | | Voluntary Church —"— | |
| | | | parade | Sm |

# WAR DIARY
## INTELLIGENCE SUMMARY

Army Form C. 2118.

*(Erase heading not required)*

Instructions regarding War Diaries and Intelligence Summaries are contained in F. S. Regs., Part II. and the Staff Manual respectively. Title pages will be prepared in manuscript.

| Place | Date | Hour | Summary of Events and Information | Remarks and references to Appendices |
|---|---|---|---|---|
| VAUCHELLES | 22.9.19 | | Orders received to send all returned men on 14 days UK leave to report on expiration of leave to 162 Bn K.R.R.C.  31 O.R demobilized | S.4.14 |
| " | 23.9.19 | | 101 O.R sent on leave to U.K. for K.R.R.C | S.4.14 |
| | | | 41 O.R demobilized to U.K | |
| " | 24.9.19 | | 63 men despatched on U.K leave for K.R.R.C. Cont.d Signing on 2 extra Coo | |
| | | | 38 " " " " " on demobilization. Presd.d 1 - L.DRAPER | |
| | | | Batt.n H.Q., Q.M. & Transport, A Coy move to No 3 AUSTRALIAN HOSPITAL ABBEVILLE | S.4.14 |
| | | | Battalion Officers Mess formed | |
| ABBEVILLE | 25.9.19 | | 15 men to U.K on leave for K.R.R.C. All Coys merged to "X" Coy 1/c of L.t DRAPER | S.4.14 |
| | | | 2.Lt G.A. STAPLEY to hospital | |
| " | 26.9.19 | | 28 " " for demobilization. Lieut LANDER - 2/Lt ENGLEBACK, CHESTERTON, C | |
| | | | 15 " " " " " MANNING MC to No 2 Postings & War Cas ABBEVILLE for temporary duty | S.4.14 |
| " | 27.9.19 | | Lieuts PRYNN & CHUDLEY to Abbev.th Sub. area H.Q. for special duty | S.4.14 |
| " | 28.9.19 | | Leave & demobilisation suspended owing to railway strike | S.4.14 |
| " | 29.9.19 | | Voluntary Church Services | S.4.14 |
| | | | Total effective strength of Men's now 22 officers and 155 O.R | S.4.14 |

## DISPOSAL OF CANTEEN FUNDS.

It has been decided to hand the balance of the Canteen Fund to the Depot of the Civil Service Rifles, at Somerset House, as a grant towards the Old Comrades Fund. This Fund is run for the benefit of all men who have served with the Civil Service Rifles, and has these two objects in view:-

(1) To assist financially, any deserving cases, and
(2) To supply funds for the periodical re-unions, concerts, &c., which will take place.

It is felt that the money will do far more good in this manner, than by making a small issue of Canteen goods to each man on his departure from the Battalion.

16.9.19.

Major, P.R.I.

Army Form C. 2118.

# WAR DIARY
## or
## INTELLIGENCE SUMMARY.
*(Erase heading not required.)*

Instructions regarding War Diaries and Intelligence Summaries are contained in F. S. Regs., Part II. and the Staff Manual respectively. Title pages will be prepared in manuscript.

| Place | Date | Hour | Summary of Events and Information | Remarks and references to Appendices |
|---|---|---|---|---|
| ABBEVILLE | 30.9.14 | | All Centre Stretcher Secs to 20th Batt. Hants Regt | foss |

J. B. L. a. H. 7/757.

The Secretary
　　War Office (SD2)
　　　London

Sir.
　　I beg to enclose herewith, War Diary of this Battalion from 1/10/19 up to the date of the Equipment with Guard proceeding to UK.

　　　　I have the honour to be, Sir
　　　　　Your obedient servant

　　　　　　Allan O'Neill
　　　　　　　Lieut.
　　　　　O.C. Equipment & Guard
　　　　　2/15 Bn. London Regt.
　　　　　(PWO. Civil Service Rifles)

19.10.19.

# WAR DIARY
## or
## INTELLIGENCE SUMMARY.
(Erase heading not required.)

Army Form C. 2118.

| Place | Date | Hour | Summary of Events and Information | Remarks and references to Appendices |
|---|---|---|---|---|
| ABBAVILLE | | | 2nd Eastern Gen. Hospt. W. Cor. B.E.F. | |
| | 1.10.19 | | All ranks of the unit inspected under Lt BURCHETT to have Rifles | |
| | | | PONT DE BRIQUES | |
| | 2.10.19 | | Court of Enquiry held on bicycles (stolen) to 30th Division. Lt DRAPER presided | S/Lt |
| | | | Unit Register Card inspected by officers from ABBEVILLE. But one MR | S/Lt |
| | 3.10.19 | | Referents to aid Post Class down | S/Lt |
| | 4.10.19 | | Medical equipment to battn inspected by S.M.O. Abbeville | S/Lt |
| | 5.10.19 | | Voluntary Church Services | S/Lt |
| | 6.10.19 | | Equipment of battalion inspected by officer detailed by Comd. Abbeville | |
| | | | Lt CVDR HUTLEY to Concentration Camp ABBEVILLE for temporary duty | S/Lt |
| | | | F.G.C.M. on Pte PRITLOVE (aban ty) 41.d c/ ABBEVILLE | S/Lt |
| | 7.10.19 | | Chaplain (Capt. Edward JCF) takes 48 hrs OR on visit to PARIS | S/Lt |
| | 8.10.19 | | No Entry for this date | S/Lt |
| | 9.10.19 | | —do— | S/Lt |
| | 10.10.19 | | —do— | S/Lt |
| | 11.10.19 | | Promulgation of Pte PRITLOVE's F.G.C.M. Awarded 140 days IHL 2/Lt CW HUTLEY reported back from Concen. Camp | |

Army Form C. 2118.

# WAR DIARY
## or
## INTELLIGENCE SUMMARY.
(Erase heading not required.)

| Place | Date | Hour | Summary of Events and Information | Remarks and references to Appendices |
|---|---|---|---|---|
| ABBEVILLE | 12.10.19 | | Voluntary Church Services. Officers reported to Labour Groups as per attached list | |
| | | | Lieut Col. Ellett D.S.O. M.C. Major Tonkin D.S.O. ordered to War Office | |
| | | | Lieut Hawkins to front of R.T.O. Calais | |
| Same Date | | | Lieutenants BURCHETT, RICHARDS, JOHNSTON, 2/Lt STAPLEY | M.S.S |
| | | | & HUTLEY respective Labour Groups. | |
| | 13.10.19 | | Lieut ANTILL proceeds to 16th Bn K.R.R.C. conducting 55 O.R. to that unit. Lieut ANTILL to then proceed to his Labour Group. | 8a.m. |
| | 14.10.19 | | 11 O.R. to U.K. for demobilization | |
| | 15.10.19 | | Lieuts NETLEY & DRAPER to Labour Groups 27 and 2 respectively. | 8 a.m. |
| | | | 12 O.R. to A.P.M. Abbeville for duty | |
| | 16.10.19 | | No entry for this date | a.m. |
| | 17.10.19 | | Order of 15.10.19 for 12 O.R. cancelled. | a.m. |
| | 18.10.19 | | 12 O.R. proceeded to join 16 K.R.R.C. at Havre 10 a.m. | a.m. |
| | | | Orders received for Equip. with Green to load by 900 men on 19/10/19 | a.m. |
| | 19.10.19 | | Equipment with Green entrained | a.m. |

Headquarters,
L. of C. Area.                                C.R.31203/O.1.

With reference to un-numbered and undated minute from O.C., 2/15th Battalion, London Regt. the officers referred to therein are disposed of as follows:-

| Lieut. | G.H.HETLEY, M.C. | No.22 Labour Group. No.1. A.Area |
| " | H.J.B.SIMON | No.21 " " No.1. " |
| " | P.DRAPER | No.2. " " No.1. " |
| " | F.H.CHUDLEY | No.76 " " No.3. " |
| " | L.G.BENNETT | No.37 " " No.3. " |
| " | W.J.BURCHETT | No.73 " " No.3. " |
| " | F.H.RICHARDS | No.73 " " No.3. " |
| " | L.M.ANTILL | No.83 " " No.3. " |
| " | G.W.PRYNN | No.83 " " No.3. " |
| " | D.A.S.MANNING, MC | No.84 " " No.3. " |
| " | L.C.LANDER | No.84 " " No.3. " |
| " | J.JOHNSTON | No.53 " " No.3. " |
| 2/Lt. | J.T.ENGLEBACK | No.21. " " No.1. " |
| " | G.A.STAPLEY, M.M. | No.76 " " No.3. " |
| " | A.K.CHESTERTON MC | No.76 " " No.3. " |
| " | G.V.D.A.HUTLEY | No.67 " " No.3. " |
| " | P.T.KEMPTON | No.67 " " No.3. " |

(DUISANS)
N°3 LaChapellette

Will you please order these Officers to proceed forthwith and join the above Labour Groups for duty.

H.Q., B.T. in F.& F.            (Sgd) W.GREY-WILSON, Major,
25-9-1919.                       for Deputy Adj. & Quartermaster Gene

-------------------------------------------------------------

O.C.,
    2/15th London Regt.                          55/914.
-----------------------

For information and necessary action.

Please report dated of departure to this office, and give reasons in case of any who may be unavailable to proceed.

H.Q.,
ABBEVILLE SUB-DISTRICT.
7-10-1919.
                                                    Major,
                                                 Staff Captain.

O.C
  2/15th London Regt.                                              73/D
-------------------------------

          The attached is returned for disposal in
accordance with GRO 7263.

                                              M Macdonald
Headquarters,                                          Lieut
Abbeville Sub-District,                         Major,
14th October, 1919.                          Staff Captain.

www.ingramcontent.com/pod-product-compliance
Lightning Source LLC
Chambersburg PA
CBHW081406160426
43193CB00013B/2116